TECHNICAL ANALYSIS & OPTIONS STRATEGIES

KENNETH H SHALEEN

PROBUS PUBLISHING COMPANY
Chicago, Illinois
Cambridge, England

ISBN 1-55738-407-X

Printed in the United States of America

BB

1 2 3 4 5 6 7 8 9 0

Dedication

To Debbie

Again

CONTENTS

Appendices

PREFACE

This book is composed primarily of case studies using actual market conditions. This approach allows a trader to view options theory in actual practice. The studies were not selected after the fact. This serves to illustrate what a technically oriented speculator would be seeing and reacting to. In some cases, the subsequent market price behavior failed to conform to the expected outcome. The case studies illustrate both the risks and rewards in using various options strategies when taking a speculative market view.

Options allow the construction of myriad trading strategies. Most books, in explaining various options positions, dismiss the problem of when to use the strategy with a simple statement along the lines of: "Normally entered when the market shows signs of increasing activity, with greater probability to the upside." The description of when to use the strategy never explains how to determine when the market is in that particular condition. The focus of this book is to highlight the technical situations that suggest when a trader should examine a particular option position.

The underlying instrument in most of the case studies in this book is a futures contract, but the classical technical aspects seen on the various charts are representative of any freely traded market. Thus, the concepts discussed are applicable to any optionable product.

The strategies selected for each technical situation do not cover the range of possible option positions, nor may they be the optimal strategies. But the case studies illustrated should certainly be thought provoking and allow for the development of techniques to suit a particular trading style.

CHAPTER 1

TECHNICAL OVERVIEW

Technical analysis involves research into the demand and supply for securities and commodities based on price studies. Technical analysts use charts or computer programs to identify and project both short and long-term price trends. Unlike fundamental analysis, technical analysis is not concerned with the financial position of a company or supply/demand statistics for a commodity.

Some forms of technical analysis, classical bar charting in particular, provide well-defined risk/reward parameters and measuring objectives. As the technician observes the evolution of a pattern, specific options strategies may be far more suitable for establishing a position than a trade of outright long or short. This is especially true in the futures markets with the propensity to gap open beyond reasonably placed protective stop-loss orders.

Because of the problems of interpretation of price, volume and open interest on an options chart, all of the technical analysis in this book will be performed on the chart of the underlying instrument.

PRICE PATTERNS

Because of the time decay inherent with options, charts of their price activity do not contain reliable price patterns for the classical bar chartist. The chart of an option that is out-of-the-money going into expiration will have a price "tail" that approaches its intrinsically worthless value of zero. At the other extreme, the deeper an option is in-the-money, the greater its price movements reflect that of the underlying instrument.

Figure 1-1 shows the bar charts of a June 70 strike price call option and its underlying instrument, a U.S. Treasury bond futures contract. A Double Bottom was activated on the T-bond chart. A selloff in early April took the T-bonds back to the underlying support at the former high of 69-00. The equivalent selloff in the June 70 call option was far more severe. The low of the selloff in the price of the call came much closer to its price low of mid-March than the simple reaction that occurred on the T-bond chart. This gave the option chart the look of a Head & Shoulders Bottom (see Chapter Four). Although classic bottoming patterns formed on both charts, they were different formations. Since the underlying instrument is the driving force behind any option's price, technical work should be concentrated on it.

Classical bar chart price pattern recognition is aimed at locating dynamic situations where market movement is expected and measuring objectives can be calculated. Thus, most of the technical analysis effort in this book attempts to identify trending or trend reversing situations as opposed to sideways or flat markets.

The strongest and most reliable price pattern is the Head & Shoulders Reversal. The theoretical underpinnings of this formation will be examined in Chapter Four. This will set the stage for the actual case studies that follow in Chapters Five, Six and Seven.

The premiere continuation pattern is the Symmetrical Triangle. The theory behind this formation is developed in Chapter Eight. Options strategies to trade a Triangle are studied in Chapters Nine and Ten.

Sometimes a market is simply trending—with a known direction, but without a specific price target. Trendline analysis in conjunction with various options strategies is explored in Chapters Eleven and Twelve.

A market undergoing a correction before continuing in the direction of the major price trend is examined in Chapter Sixteen. This is where a technician who is comfortable with an Elliott Wave count on a chart can earn premium income in a net sideways market environment.

VOLUME

Technicians typically use volume (turnover) to measure the urgency associated with a price move. In an equity market, volume on an individual stock (not its option) is relatively stable. Analysis is straightforward. In a futures market, volume on an individual futures contract (not its option) experiences an increase as it becomes the lead contract and then declines going into expiration. This effect is damped out by using total futures volume (all contracts).

In an options market, volume is simply the number of options contracts traded each trading session. The analysis problem with volume of an individual option is that an option does not necessarily exhibit a normal volume escalation and then a severe decline as expiration approaches. Many options expire out-of-the-money and no offsetting action is needed. There is no easy method of isolating the effects on volume that are simply due to the contract specifications.

Figure 1-1   **Different Price Patterns**

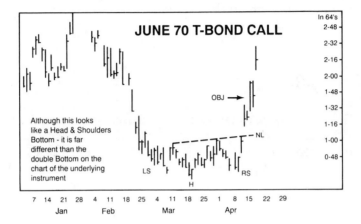

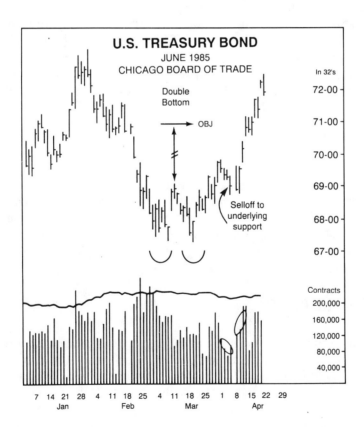

Figure 1-2 illustrates total options volume and the total volume on its underlying instrument (soybean futures). Although a high correlation in the two volume plots is observable, volume analysis in this book will be performed on the underlying instrument only.

OPEN INTEREST

Open interest (OI) in either an options market or futures market is the summation of all unclosed purchases or sales at the end of a trading session. The long open interest is always equal to the short open interest. The published open interest figure represents one side of the trade only.

Open interest yields a good insight (in conjunction with volume) as to the liquidity in a particular options series. The question is: Can open interest changes in options be used by technicians in the same analytical fashion as on a futures chart? The answer is no.

Open interest in a specific option, such as the XYZ June 100 call, is influenced to an inordinate extent by the price of the underlying XYZ instrument. Even adding the open interest of the XYZ June 100 put or summing the open positions of all XYZ June puts and calls will not produce a plot that can be easily analyzed.

The configuration of total open interest on an options chart is most analogous to the configuration of open interest on a cash-settled futures chart. There is a technique for removing the trend component of open interest increase in a cash-settled futures contract. This must be done on the S&P 500 futures and the popular (worldwide) Eurodollar Time Deposit futures. But even using this technique on options does not produce satisfactory results.*

Figure 1-2 shows the total open interest plot of all the options trading on soybean futures and the total futures open interest. A technician readily notes the difference between the two plots. Futures open interest exhibits a fairly stable nature. In contrast is the regular escalation and precipitous drop in the options open interest.

PUT/CALL RATIO

The investing public trader favors buying options rather than writing options, for obvious risk reasons. The U.S. stock market is also the public trader's favorite market. The put/call ratio in equity options is used in a contrary sense. If put volume is too high in relation to call volume, the public

*An in-depth analysis of futures markets statistics is found in *Volume and Open Interest: Cutting Edge Strategies in the Futures Markets*, Probus 1991.

**Figure 1-2   Volume and Open Interest
Option and Underlying Instrument**

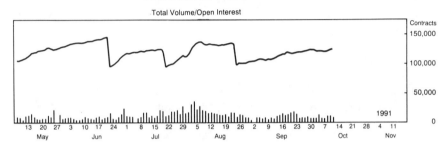

SOYBEAN OPTIONS

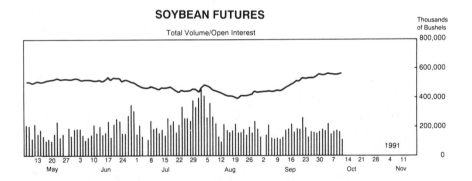

SOYBEAN FUTURES

is deemed to be very bearish. Using the theory that the masses will always be wrong, a bullish reading results.

This tool does merit consideration in the equity options market, but it is not of great use in options on futures. Hedging concerns of commercial users often dominate the usage of puts or calls. In addition, there is the problem of whether to use the *number* of puts to calls or the *dollar value* of puts to calls. Consequently, traditional analysis of the volume on the underlying instrument will be the norm in all of the case studies.

WHEN TO ENTER A TRADE

The age-old question any trader faces is when to enter a new position. The three most obvious choices for a classical bar chartist are:

1. In anticipation of a breakout

2. On the breakout (a close outside the formation)

3. On a price pullback toward the breakout

Suggested answers would incorporate the following:

1. Discipline is a key for any trading strategy. Technicians often see a potential pattern developing and want to lead off—establishing an outright long or short position prior to the breakout. This is a dangerous practice. An options trade can often be designed with a limited risk parameter, anticipating the breakout. The position must be easily liquidated if it is incorrect (a breakout does not occur) or if volume (and open interest if underlying instrument is a futures contract) does not validate the breakout.

2. The options position should be easily converted to a more aggressive directional position on the breakout. Some option strategies, by definition, become more aggressive as the anticipated price move occurs.

3. If a pullback to the breakout/pattern occurs, the trader should be able to adjust the options position to an even greater aggressive directional stance. The resulting strategy must have an identifiable risk parameter. The specific stop-out point would normally be derived from trendlines or support/resistance analysis on the chart of the underlying instrument.

After the traditional technical analysis has been accomplished, an options strategy can be selected to take advantage of the anticipated price move. The position can be fine-tuned if the trader is familiar with important options characteristics such as volatility and delta and understands how they would change under both favorable and unfavorable price moves.

For a technical trader, however, determining the direction and expected magnitude of the price move is paramount. Many of the nuances of options theory are quickly overpowered if the price moves quickly toward the expected measuring objective.

CHAPTER 2

OPTIONS STRATEGY MATRIX

The strategy matrix on the next several pages summarizes the content of this book. The column labeled Technical Situation is the key. The first two columns are standard options positions and the price environment in which they should be used. Once a specific technical aspect on a chart has been identified, the matrix is used to help select and implement an options strategy. The case studies then monitor the subsequent price activity and technical developments. Any required adjustments (follow-up activity) to the initial options position are made and the eventual outcome noted.

After the reader has examined the individual case studies, the strategy matrix should serve as a useful starting place or guide when a current trade is being contemplated.

The divisional headings within the matrix subdivide it into five major technical categories. For the reasons detailed in Chapter One, the directional positions encompass the majority of the strategies.

The case studies beginning in Chapter Five illustrate one or more specific technical situations. These case study chapters each begin with the relevant row in the options strategy matrix:

Option Strategy	When to Use	Technical Situation

Technical Analysis and Options Strategy Matrix

Directional Positions

Option Strategy	When to Use	Technical Situation
Long Call	When most bullish	En route to price pattern measuring objective after pullback has occurred
Synthetic Long Call	When most bullish	A gap open is likely to exceed a normal futures sell-stop order (report due)
Short Call	Firmly believe market is not going up	Within Descending Right Triangle or after Double Top has been activated and volatility has increased dramatically
Long Put	When most bearish	En route to price pattern measuring objective after pullback has occurred
Synthetic Long Put	When most bearish	A gap open is likely to exceed a normal futures buy-stop order (report due)
Short Put	Firmly believe market is not going down	Within Ascending Right Triangle or in situation where implied volatility is too high to justify long call position
Vertical Bull Call Spread	Market expected to go up somewhat	Lead off in anticipation of upside breakout (prior to breaking neckline of a possible H&S Bottom)
Vertical Bear Put Spread	Market expected to fall somewhat	Lead off in anticipation of downside breakout (prior to breaking neckline of a possible H&S Top)
Call Ratio Back Spread	Greater probability market will move to upside	Within Symmetrical Triangle in a bull market
Put Ratio Back Spread	Greater probability market will move to downside	Within Symmetrical Triangle in a bear market

Estimating Expiration Price of Underlying Instrument

Option Strategy	When to Use	Technical Situation
Long Butterfly	Conservative trade using long-term options series	When measuring objective can be obtained from a weekly chart
Calendar Spread (Long Time Spread)	Sideways market near term—then resuming major trend	In Elliott Wave II or IV. Major trend up: calls. Major trend down: puts (closest OTM series used)

Large move in *either* direction when close to expiration

Short Butterfly	Immediate move expected	1. Converging trendlines 2. Within Symmetrical Triangle
Vertical Credit Spread	Directional Bias close to expiration	Minor trend change indicator

Large move in either direction when farther from expiration

Long Straddle	Immediate move expected	1. Within Symmetrical Triangle 2. Testing a trendline 3. Cluster of closes 4. Open interest increasing dramatically

Flat Market

Short Straddle	Expect stagnating price activity	1. Volume and open interest declining
Short Strangle	Market going sideways and stagnating	2. Triangle forming on weekly chart 3. In Elliott Wave II or IV
Neutral Calendar Spread	Expect stagnating price activity	4. In-between support and resistance

Note: Often the initial options strategy will be altered as subsequent price activity is entered on the chart. This may involve removing one-half of the losing leg of a spread at the breakout and the remaining one-half on a pullback. Thus, a minimum of two contracts per leg is a desirable starting strategy.

CHAPTER 3

VERTICAL SPREADS

A *vertical spread* in options is probably the most classic strategy of taking a view on expected market movement. Vertical spreads are extremely useful to technical traders. They can be used to lead off in anticipation of a price move. This is especially true for a classical bar chartist who is expecting a traditional price pattern to be set off. This chapter will examine this versatile options strategy from a theoretical standpoint and introduce risk/reward diagrams.

A vertical spread consists of either call or put options with the same expiration date but different strike prices. The vertical spread derived its name because options having the same expiration date are listed in the U.S. financial newspapers in the same vertical column. Strike prices dictate the horizontal rows.

BULL SPREAD

A vertical bull spread is constructed by buying (long) an option with a lower strike and selling (short) a higher strike option of the same type and expiration. The bull spread can utilize either calls for both legs of the spread *or* puts for both legs of the spread. This type of spread should be profitable in a market in which the underlying instrument is trending higher in price.

The decision as to which strikes to select will be based on the measuring objective obtained from the technical analysis. Liquidity considerations will also be important because follow-up action is anticipated as the expected price move develops. This dynamic aspect of restructuring the initial options strategy will be covered in great detail in the various case studies.

Debit Spread

Using calls for both legs of a vertical bull spread creates a *debit spread*. Funds are debited from the trader's account to pay for the spread. One of the benefits to a nonprofessional trader using a debit spread is that the amount of funds removed from the account represents the maximum risk. The net debit is equal to the amount paid for (buying) the lower strike call minus the amount received for (selling) the higher strike call.

Even if the trader is 180 degrees off in market direction, the net debit (and the ever-present commissions) still represents the maximum loss. Thus, a trader is unlikely to be called for margin.* This representation of a nonprofessional trader may sound harsh, but casual participants in the serious world of trading tend to lose much more than reasonably expected. A debit spread provides "staying power" and a known risk parameter.

Another benefit of using call options in a vertical bull spread is that it facilitates follow-up action as the expected bull market develops. The specific characteristics of this versatile options spread are detailed in Table 3-1. The vertical bull call spread will be investigated in Chapter Five in conjunction with a developing Head & Shoulders Bottom price pattern.

Table 3-1   Characteristics of a Vertical Bull Call Spread

1. Long lower strike call versus short higher strike call

2. Limited risk and limited reward

3. Debit transaction

4. Breakeven = lower strike + net debit

5. Maximum profit = higher strike − lower strike − net debit

6. Maximum loss = net debit

7. Margin = amount paid (net debit)

Credit Spread

A vertical bull spread placed for a credit uses put options for both legs. The lower strike remains the long leg of the spread. The net credit taken in represents the maximum reward. The difference between the strikes minus the credit is the maximum loss.

Credit spreads are popular strategies for professional traders who desire to bring funds into their (interest-bearing) accounts. The spread is placed to

---

* The possibility of early exercise on the short leg of a vertical spread is detailed at the end of this chapter.

take advantage of time decay as well as market direction. In a vertical bull put spread, the premium received for selling the higher strike is greater than the premium paid for buying the lower strike. If the underlying instrument is above the higher strike at expiration, both put options will expire worthless and the trader gets to keep the credit received. This technique is covered in detail in Chapter Fourteen.

RISK/REWARD DIAGRAMS

Since most technical analysis is graphically oriented, a technically based options trader should be at ease with risk/reward (profit/loss) diagrams. For the basic options strategies presented in this book, the risk/reward diagrams show at a glance the range of possible outcomes if the initial options strategy is held until expiration. It should be noted, however, that in many of the case studies, subsequent market price movement dictated that the original position be modified. This is not a problem. A new risk/reward diagram should be constructed.

To introduce the subject, Figure 3-1 shows the simple, positively sloped 45-degree line of an outright long position in an underlying instrument. This would typically be long 100 shares of a stock or long 1 futures contract. The open-ended arrows are what is important. They depict unlimited risk and unlimited reward. Technically, the risk of a long position is not unlimited on the short side because the future or equity can go only to zero, not below.

Figure 3-2 is the risk/reward diagram of several vertical bull call spreads at expiration. The big differences between Figures 3-1 and 3-2 are the two discontinuities in the lines in Figure 3-2. The bend in the lines to the horizontal represents the beginning price at which risk or reward is maximized.

The vertical bull spread using call options always entails the purchase of a lower strike price call and the short sale of a higher strike price call. By varying the strikes, or the distance between the legs of the spread, different risk/reward scenarios can be created. In Figure 3-2, the current price of the underlying instrument is exactly at the price level of "C," which also happens to be the price at which an option strike is listed.

The call option with the strike price at "C" is referred to as an at-the-money (ATM) option. The vertical bull call spread can be constructed by using in-the-money (ITM), ATM or out-of-the-money (OTM) options. This will change the strategy from least aggressive to most aggressive with respect to the expected price up move. Measuring objectives obtained from the price chart of the underlying and liquidity considerations will dictate which option strikes to select. The choice of which strikes and expiration to use will be covered in detail in Chapters Four and Five.

Figure 3-1   Risk/Reward Diagram of a Long Position in the Underlying Instrument

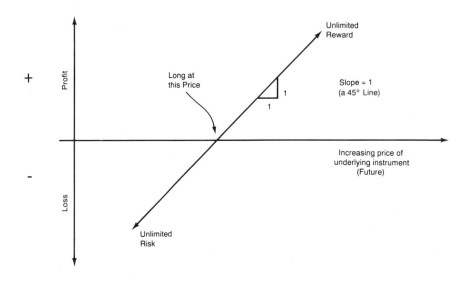

In looking at Figure 3-2, it is important to note that the maximum profit in a vertical bull call spread is realized if the price of the underlying is at or above the higher strike at expiration. The maximum loss is recorded if the underlying is at or below the lower strike at expiration. These concepts will become second nature very soon after any options trading program is begun.

New options traders are encouraged to plot the risk/reward strategies of the simple spreads presented in this book. In fact, close examination of the risk/reward diagrams in the case studies will reveal that the same chart paper and grid values are used to construct both the price plot of the underlying instrument and the risk/reward diagrams. A discussion of how to create a tabular risk/reward matrix and the resulting risk/reward diagram is found in Chapter Five; refer to Table 5-5 and Figure 5-9.

BEAR SPREAD

A vertical bear spread is constructed by buying a higher strike and selling a lower strike option, both of the same type and expiration. Puts can be used

Figure 3-2   Risk/Reward Diagrams of Vertical Bull Call Spreads at Expiration

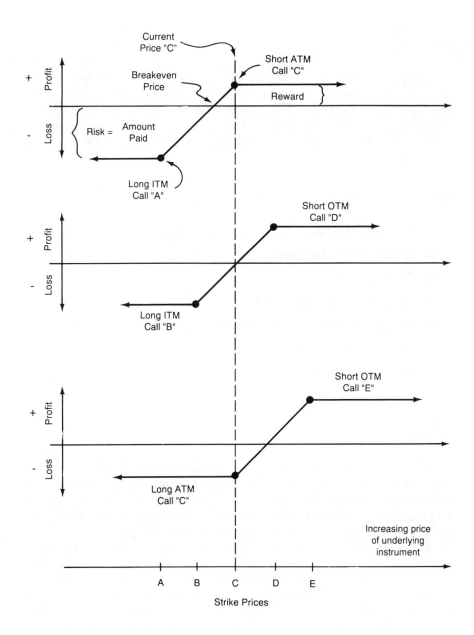

for both legs of the spread or calls can be used. The vertical bear spread should be profitable in a downtrending price market.

Debit Spread

Utilizing put options in a vertical bear spread creates a debit spread. This strategy allows for follow-up action as the expected price down move develops. The vertical bear put spread will be investigated in Chapter Seven as a strategy for leading off in anticipation of a Head & Shoulders Top forming on a chart. The important characteristics of this spread are found in Table 3-2.

Table 3-2   Characteristics of a Vertical Bear Put Spread

1. Long higher strike put versus short lower strike put

2. Limited risk and limited reward

3. Debit transaction

4. Breakeven = higher strike – net debit

5. Maximum profit = higher strike – lower strike – net debit

6. Maximum loss = net debit

7. Margin = amount paid (net debit)

Credit Spread

A bearish view can also be adopted by options traders desiring to write a spread for a credit using calls for both legs of the spread. The higher strike remains the long leg. The maximum reward is the credit received. The maximum loss is equal to the distance between the legs of the spread (converted to Dollars per contract) minus the net credit.

As with the credit bull spread, follow-up action from a credit bear spread is not as advantageous as in the debit spread. This is especially true for a trader expecting a substantial price move but desiring the liquidity of at-the-money options. Therefore, the debit spreads (both bull and bear) will be the predominant examples in this book. This does not mean that credit spreads are not a powerful tool. A vertical bear spread using call options is examined in Chapter Fourteen.

DECAY OF VERTICAL SPREADS WITH TIME

The risk/reward diagrams of vertical spreads at expiration are straightforward, but the spreads are obviously initiated at price differences off that
curve. How does the value of a debit vertical spread change over time?
Options pricing suggests the following:*

In-the-money	Bull Call Spreads and Bear Put Spreads	Gain in value most sharply in last 30 market days
Out-of-the-money	Bull Call Spreads and Bear Put Spreads	Lose value most sharply in last 30 market days

The movement of a spread's value toward the inevitable location some-
where on the risk/reward line at expiration is known as the decaying
process. This is shown in Figure 3-3. The conclusion is that if the anticipated
price move does not begin as soon as the trader expected (and prices remain
flat), the in-the-money spreads make time work for the spreader.

Figure 3-3   Decay of a Vertical Bull Call Spread with Time

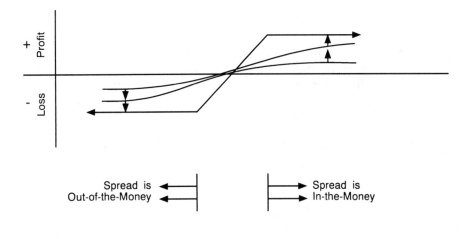

---

* Refer to Appendix B for an overview of a representative options pricing model.

ADDITIONAL OPTIONS CONSIDERATIONS

1. Options terminology can be very confusing. This is evident when traders refer to being long or short a particular spread. A standard convention used is that any spread initiated at a debit is referred to as a long position.

2. All of the options spread strategies presented in this book are assumed to be initiated as spreads. The execution will occur on a single order ticket. "Legging into" a spread by trying to outguess short-term market direction is day trading. The technical situations being analyzed are to be exploited by a position trading approach. An example of a spread order ticket can be seen in Figure 12-2.

3. A general rule of thumb used in selecting which spread to buy or sell would take into consideration whether implied volatility is judged to be high or low when the spread is initiated. If implied volatility is high (and likely to decline), theoretical options pricing theory suggests that better value will be obtained by concentrating on selling the at-the-money option leg of the spread. If implied volatility is deemed to be low, purchase of at-the-money options is favored.* Volatility forecasting is addressed in Chapter Fifteen.

4. An options spreader must be aware if early exercise is a possibility that could disrupt the trade. A debit spread does not contain an inordinate amount of early exercise risk. The long leg of the spread will be farther in the money than the short leg. Economic rationale dictates early exercise only when an option is very far in-the-money. This is another reason for using calls in a vertical bull spread`(and puts in a vertical bear spread).

5. All of the case studies in this book use American-style options, which means that the long can exercise at any time up to expiration. This factor, however, will not play an important role in any of the strategies selected.

* Figure C-2 in Appendix C illustrates this aspect of the option pricing model.

CHAPTER 4

THEORETICAL EXAMPLE—HEAD & SHOULDERS BOTTOM

To set the stage for the case studies in the following chapters, Chapter Four examines the theoretical underpinnings of the Head & Shoulders Reversal formation. This chapter presents a decision tree for several of the most distinct price moves that might occur after a technician spots a possible Head & Shoulders Bottom developing. An initial options strategy is formulated and follow-up action is suggested depending on subsequent price activity.

The Head & Shoulders (H&S) Reversal formation is the strongest and most reliable classical chart pattern. When properly formed with the ideal volume considerations, it has a reliability of success in achieving its measuring objective in excess of 80 percent.

Figure 4-1 illustrates a price chart of an underlying instrument on which a Head & Shoulders Bottom may be forming. Implementation of an options trading strategy occurs after the fifth reversal of the minor price trend on a chart. This is *prior to* the neckline being broken to the upside and the pattern being officially activated by a high volume close above the neckline.

The suggested options position is a vertical bull call spread. A minimum of two options on each leg of the spread is necessary to allow for enough follow-up action.

DECISION TREE

Figure 4-1 shows the minimum amount of price development that must occur on a chart before implementing an options trading strategy based

---

Figure 4-1   Possible Head & Shoulders Bottom

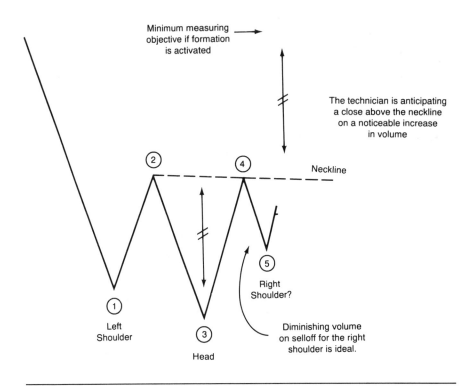

Minimum measuring ——▶
objective if formation
is activated

The technician is anticipating
a close above the neckline
on a noticeable increase
in volume

② ④   Neckline

⑤

Right
Shoulder?

①

Left
Shoulder   Diminishing volume
on selloff for the right
③   shoulder is ideal.

Head

---

upon a possible Head & Shoulders pattern. This is the starting node for the decision tree in Figure 4-2. Moving down in the decision tree, a trader encounters some of the possible paths and the trading decisions that must be made along the way.

The uppermost figure in the decision tree, labeled decision node 1, shows call options strike prices. They are labeled A through E and range from an in-the-money (ITM) call at a strike price of A to an out-of-the-money (OTM) call with a strike price of E. The call option with a strike closest to the tick mark of the current closing price of the underlying instrument is the at-the-money (ATM) call C.

Decision Node 1: Initiate Trade

The trading strategy begins with leading off by placing a position in anticipation that the possible Head & Shoulders Bottom will be activated. This is a

Figure 4-2   Decision Tree: Possible Head & Shoulders Bottom

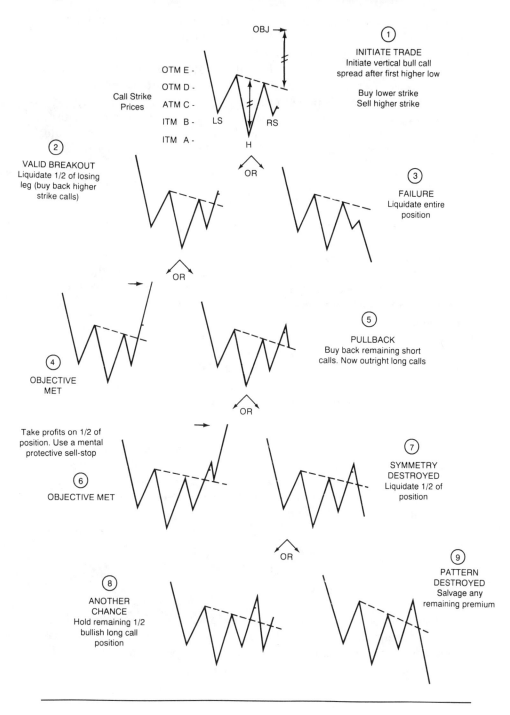

OBJ →

OTM E -
OTM D -
ATM C -
ITM B -
ITM A -

Call Strike Prices

LS   RS

H

①
INITIATE TRADE
Initiate vertical bull call
spread after first higher low

Buy lower strike
Sell higher strike

OR

②
VALID BREAKOUT
Liquidate 1/2 of losing
leg (buy back higher
strike calls)

③
FAILURE
Liquidate entire
position

OR

④
OBJECTIVE
MET

⑤
PULLBACK
Buy back remaining short
calls. Now outright long calls

OR

Take profits on 1/2 of
position. Use a mental
protective sell-stop

⑥
OBJECTIVE MET

⑦
SYMMETRY
DESTROYED
Liquidate 1/2 of
position

OR

⑧
ANOTHER
CHANCE
Hold remaining 1/2
bullish long call
position

⑨
PATTERN
DESTROYED
Salvage any
remaining premium

vertical bull call spread. Lower strike calls are purchased and higher strike calls are sold.

An approximate upside measuring objective can be obtained at this time. This would imply placing a vertical bull call spread with the highest strike at the measuring objective. It is suggested, however, that the closest out-of-the-money calls be purchased and the calls one strike higher be sold. This is for liquidity considerations in anticipation of follow-up action when the neckline (just overhead) is penetrated.

The next lower level in the decision tree shows the two most distinct price moves that could occur—a rally or a selloff. The market also could move sideways or experience myriad other price gyrations.

Decision Node 2: Valid Breakout

A close above the neckline on a noticeable increase in volume officially activates the H&S Bottom. This allows the technician to construct the specific upside measuring objective. It is also the time to make any trading strategy more directionally aggressive. For a vertical bull call spread, one-half of the losing leg should be liquidated. This means buying back—covering—one-half of the higher strike calls that were sold short.

It is of utmost importance for any trader to have a defined risk parameter. For classical bar chartists, this is usually straightforward. Assuming there was no possible second left shoulder on the chart, the technician would not expect the low of the right shoulder to be taken out. Thus, the bullish outlook would not seriously deteriorate unless a selloff to below the right shoulder occurred.

Stop-loss orders in the options themselves are not usually recommended. A "mental" stop in the underlying instrument is the preferred approach. This means, of course, that a trader must possess the discipline to exit from a losing options position if the technical aspects of the underlying instrument begin breaking down.

Decision Node 3: Failure

Any Head & Shoulders formation is destroyed when the extreme of the head is violated, even intraday. This is the path taken in decision node 3. Any bull strategy must be abandoned. The entire vertical bull spread should be liquidated.

Making a new price low affirms that the direction of the major trend remains downward. It does not automatically create a specific downside measuring objective. Therefore, it is never advisable to liquidate the long calls and stay with the short calls of the vertical spread. The position would turn into one of unlimited risk. It is far better to exit from a losing position and look for another more clear-cut technical situation.

Decision Node 4: Objective Met

When any classical bar charting measuring objective is met, it is prudent to realize at least some profits. In the case of the Head & Shoulders formation, profits on one-quarter to one-half of the position should be taken. Why only 25 percent? An H&S measuring objective is a *minimum* target. Although no specific maximum objective can be calculated, quotes often move far beyond the minimum objective.

A trader should try to follow the old adage of cutting losses and letting profits run. This is what is being done in removing only a portion of the winning trade. The decision to exit from the remaining open positions should be based on usual support/resistance and volume/open interest considerations.

Decision Node 5: Pullback

In the long run, the most optimal path through the decision tree would flow through decision node 5. A price sell-off on declining volume back to the neckline would prompt removal of any remaining bearish positions. All short calls should be covered. The resulting position is simply long call options. Note that this is the technical situation in the options strategy matrix in Chapter Two that results in the long call strategy. This occurs "en route to price pattern measuring objective after a pullback has occurred."

Decision Node 6: Objective Met

Similar to decision node 4, a trader should begin to take partial profits when an objective is achieved. Removing 25 to 50 percent of all bullish positions is suggested. But this is, as economists are wont to say, "all other things being equal." This is not usually the case. For example, if the underlying instrument is a futures contract, open interest changes become important. In a futures contract, open interest declining as a price target is being achieved is a warning signal. The percentage of profitable positions removed would move up to 75 percent.

In general, protective mental sell-stops in the underlying instrument would follow the market up—moving in fits and starts depending upon where support formed on the chart.

Decision Node 7: Symmetry Destroyed

If quotes move below the right shoulder low, the symmetry of the Head & Shoulders Bottom is destroyed. This does not automatically invalidate the pattern. The pattern is destroyed if the low of the head is taken out. But a trader must begin to mitigate the loss of the long call position. Removing approximately one-half of the long calls would accomplish this.

Decision Node 8: Another Chance

Since the Head & Shoulders Bottom remains valid, the original upside measuring objective is intact. A bullish stance should be held unless the low of this second pullback is taken out. The decision to add to bull positions is tricky. A close above the neckline once again would certainly revive the bullish look of the chart. Aggressive traders can then look to increase a bullish bias—possibly with outright longs in the underlying instrument rather than long calls.

Decision Node 9: Pattern Destroyed

The worst path through the decision tree culminates in decision node 9; the H&S pattern has failed. Although the H&S formation is usually highly reliable, it does fail in up to 20 percent of the cases.

If enough premium is remaining in the long call options, they can be liquidated. If so little premium remains, they can be held rather than paying commissions. Maybe the trader will get lucky and a price rally will occur. But a trader who uses the words "luck" or "hope" is in a terrible situation!

WHICH OPTIONS EXPIRATION TO USE

Timing is a critical factor for all options traders. The question of which options expiration series to use is addressed by the time frame in which the expected price move should occur. Price patterns generate minimum measuring objectives but they typically do not produce a specific time parameter of when the price target will be reached. The Head & Shoulders formation, however, does yield a reasonable *maximum* time in which the objective should be met.

A *fail-safe trendline* can be constructed using any H&S Top or Bottom formation. This trendline is drawn tangent to the price extremes of the head and right shoulder. An example is shown in Figure 4-3. A penetration (even intraday) of the fail-safe trendline is often used by technicians as a signal to liquidate outright long or short positions (i.e., positions with unlimited risk). Classical bar chartists realize that a price move beyond the extreme price in the head would officially destroy the H&S pattern. So it is possible that an

---

Figure 4-3   Intersection of Objective Price and Fail-Safe Trendline

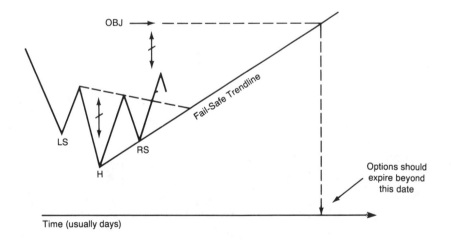

H&S formation can work even if the fail-safe trendline is broken, as long as the head is not taken out.

Figure 4-3 shows the intersection of the price height measuring objective and the fail-safe trendline. Moving down to the time scale, a date is obtained. The assumption is made that the minimum measuring objective will be achieved without violating the fail-safe trendline. This is a reasonable assumption. Hence, an options expiration at (or slightly later than) the derived date would be used.

Historical observation has shown that the price move away from a Head & Shoulders formation often accelerates. For this reason, the intersection date derived in Figure 4-3 is indeed a maximum. The measuring objective would be expected to be reached much sooner than this maximum date.

CHAPTER 5

POSSIBLE COMPLEX HEAD & SHOULDERS BOTTOM

VERTICAL BULL CALL SPREAD

Options Strategy	When to Use	Technical Situation
Vertical Bull Call Spread	Market expected to go up somewhat	Lead off in anticipation of upside breakout (prior to breaking neckline of a possible H&S Bottom)

This case study involves the amazing unfolding of major Complex Head & Shoulders Bottoms on many of the world equity index charts in late 1990 and early 1991. The word complex is used in conjunction with the price pattern because of the possible two or more left shoulders that might lead to the formation of two or more right shoulders.

Options on the Standard & Poor's (S&P) 500 Index future trade on the Index and Options Market (IOM)—a division of the Chicago Mercantile Exchange. They will be used to illustrate the power and flexibility of the vertical spread as an options trading strategy. The contract specifications for the S&P 500 futures options are listed in Table 5-1.

Case Study 1: December 1990 S&P 500

A small Head & Shoulders (H&S) Bottom was activated via an upside breakout (a close above the neckline) on the Dec S&P 500 Stock Index futures chart on November 9, 1990. Figure 5-1 shows that volume and the open interest change were not ideal on the actual breakout price posting. This

Table 5-1   Contract Specifications for the S&P 500 Futures Options

CONTRACT HIGHLIGHTS[1]

	S&P 500 Futures	Options on S&P 500 Futures
Ticker Symbol	SP	Calls: CS Puts: PS
Contract Size	$500 X S&P 500 Stock Index	One S&P 500 futures contract
Strike Prices	N/A	See note[2]
Minimum Price Fluctuation	.05 index points = $25.00	.05 index points = $25.00 per contract (A trade may occur at a nominal price if it results in liquidation for both parties of deep-out-of-the-money positions.)
Trading Hours (Chicago Time)	8:30 am-3:15 pm	
Contract Months	March, June, September, December	All 12 calendar months (The underlying instrument for the 3 monthly option expirations within a quarter is the quarter-end futures contract.)
Last Day of Trading	The business day immediately preceding the day of determination of the Final Settlement Price (normally, the Thursday prior to the 3rd Friday of the contract month).	Mar, Jun, Sep, Dec: same date as underlying futures contract. Other 8 months: the 3rd Friday of contract month

Quarterly Futures & Options Settlement Procedures:
Cash settlement. All open positions at the close of the final trading day are settled in cash to the Special Opening Quotation on Friday morning of the S&P 500 Stock Price Index.

[1]Contract specifications are subject to change without notice. Check with your broker to confirm this information.

[2]Strike price increments vary per contract month. Refer to contract specifications for specific requirements.

"S&P," "Standard & Poor's" and "S&P 500" are trademarks of the Standard and Poor's Corporation, which assumes no liability in connection with the trading of any contract based on indexes.

implies a pullback to test the neckline is likely. This H&S Bottom was confirmed by the Dow Jones Industrial Average (DJIA) chart (Figure 5-2) with a similar chart pattern and its upside breakout November 12, 1990.

Technicians were well aware of the price selloff and rally on the two equity charts back in late August. This implied that a price decline to form an outer right shoulder might occur. Any pullback to the initial breakout (313.50 on the December S&P 500 chart) particularly after a further price rally, would create the symmetry necessary for the formation of a much larger H&S Bottom pattern. Conservative traders would wait for a price selloff (pullback toward the neckline) to establish vertical bull call spreads. This position would serve to lead off on the development of a Complex Head & Shoulders Bottom on the December S&P 500 chart.

Pullback: Initiate Vertical Bull Call Spread

Friday, November 16, 1990

A price decline did occur. This can be seen on the December S&P 500 chart in Figure 5-3. Note that the price posting on Friday, November 16 includes a selloff to close a Breakaway Gap followed by a higher close. Two classical bar charting price patterns exist. The upside measuring objectives of a Symmetrical Triangle (337.70) and "inner" H&S Bottom (339.00) forecast that the much larger Complex H&S Bottom formation will be activated. This would entail a high volume (55,000+) close above the larger neckline.

Which Expiration Month to Use

The December option series on the S&P 500 future expires in five weeks (on the open on Friday, December 21). A helpful visual reminder of this date is the placement of a small arrow on the calendar scale of the chart. This is illustrated in Figure 5-3 and will be a convention used throughout this book.

The most steeply up-sloping trendline that can be constructed on the chart intersects at a price level of 331.75 on the expiration date of the December options. Assuming that this trendline will not be violated yields a minimum price expectation for the December future (and therefore the December options) at expiration. Thus, the H&S Bottom measuring objective of 339.00 does not necessarily have to be achieved by December 21. If the formation remains viable at the December option expiration, a bull strategy will be formed using the March option series.

Figure 5-1   Possible Complex Head & Shoulders Bottom

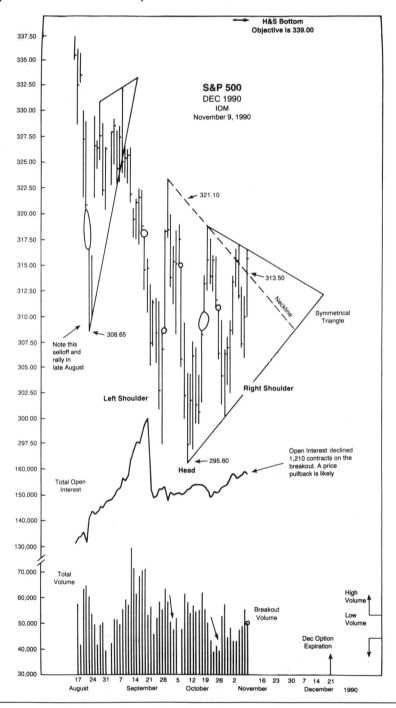

Figure 5-2   Head & Shoulders Bottom

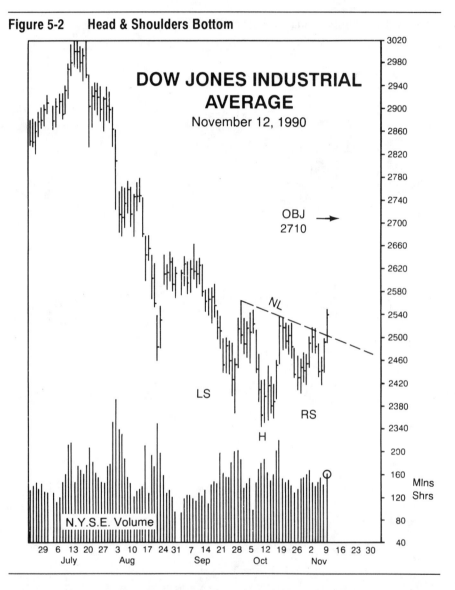

Prices for several important U.S. equity options contracts at the close on November 16 are shown in Table 5-2. Monthly (serial) options expirations do exist on the S&P 500 futures. But the January option series (which uses the March future as its underlying instrument) is not very liquid. In fact, *The Wall Street Journal* quotes in Table 5-2 do not even list prices for the January futures options! Thus, for liquidity considerations, a futures options trader would establish vertical bull call spreads in the December options.

Risk/reward diagrams for three vertical bull call spreads are shown in Figure 5-4. An initial position of buying two 320 December S&P 500 calls

Figure 5-3   Pullback: Initiate Vertical Bull Call Spreads

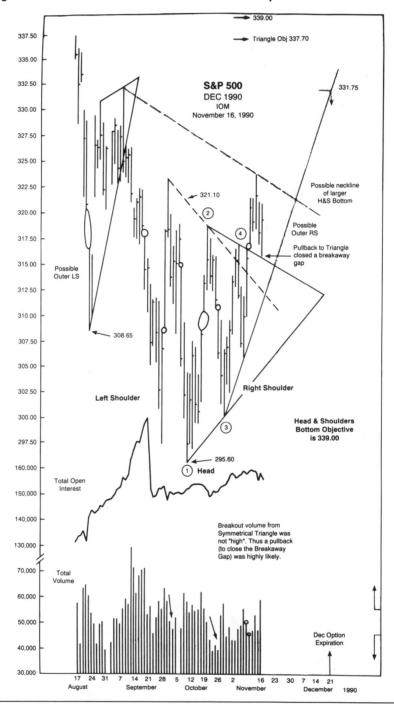

Table 5-2 Index Trading, Friday, November 16, 1990

OPTIONS

Chicago Board

S&P 100 INDEX

Strike Price	Calls—Last Nov	Calls—Last Dec	Calls—Last Jan	Puts—Last Nov	Puts—Last Dec	Puts—Last Jan
265	37⅜	40	41⅛	....	15/16	2⅝
270	32	35⅛	36⅜	....	1 3/16	3⅛
275	27⅜	30½	31¾	1/16	1 7/16	3¾
280	20⅞	24¼	26½	1/16	1⅞	4¾
285	17½	19½	....	1/16	2½	5¾
290	12½	17	20	1/16	3¼	6⅛
295	7½	12¾	18	1/16	4¼	8⅝
300	2½	9⅜	13½	1/16	5½	9½
305	1/16	6¼	10	2½	7½	12
310	1/16	3⅞	7⅛	7½	10½	15¼
315	1/16	2⅛	5¼	12½	15¼	17¼
320	1/16	1⅛	3½	18¼	18½	21¼
325	....	11/16	....	24¾	....	....
330	....	5/16	....	....	30	....
335	....	3/16	....	....	....	....
340	....	⅛	....	38⅛	....	....
350	....	1/16	....	....	....	....

Total call volume 213,384 Total call open int. 473,384
Total put volume 192,499 Total put open int. 572,709
The index: High 302.79; Low 299.24; Close 302.46, +1.08

S&P 500 INDEX

Strike Price	Calls—Last Nov	Calls—Last Dec	Calls—Last Mar	Puts—Last Nov	Puts—Last Dec	Puts—Last Mar
250	....	68	....	....	¼	2¼
275	44	....	48⅛	....	11/16	5
280	35¾	....	....	....	15/16	5⅞
285	....	....	....	....	1 3/16	....
290	....	....	....	....	1½	7⅝
295	....	25⅜	....	....	1⅞	8⅝
300	16⅛	⅝	29	1/16	2¾	10
305	12⅛	16⅝	....	1/16	3¼	11⅜
310	7⅛	13⅛	....	1/16	4¾	12⅞
315	2	8⅞	....	1/16	6¼	14⅛
320	1/16	6⅜	15¾	2⅞	8⅜	16½
325	....	4	14¾	9¼	11¼	....
330	1/16	2⅛	10½	13½	14⅞	21⅛
335	....	1¼	....	....	18⅝	....
340	....	9/16	....	23¾	22⅜	25½
345	....	5/16	5	....	27¼	30½
350	⅛	....	3⅜	....	31⅝	31⅝
355	⅛	....	....	....	37	....
360	1/16	....	....	....	....	....
365	....	....	1⅜	....	46¾	....
375	....	....	....	....	54⅝	....
380	....	....	....	....	59⅝	....

Total call volume 36,300 Total call open int. 414,893
Total put volume 49,599 Total put open int. 553,412
The index: High 318.80; Low 314.99; Close 317.12, +0.10

American Exchange

MAJOR MARKET INDEX

Strike Price	Calls—Last Nov	Calls—Last Dec	Calls—Last Jan	Puts—Last Nov	Puts—Last Dec	Puts—Last Jan
440	92⅛	....	96⅛	....	⅝	2
450	....	....	....	....	....	2⅞
460	....	....	....	....	1	....
470	....	66⅝	....	....	1⅜	4½
475	....	....	....	....	1½	....
480	55¼	....	....	....	1¾	....
490	43½	....	....	....	2 11/16	7
495	....	....	....	....	3⅛	7⅝
500	33½	37	....	....	3¼	....
505	....	....	....	1/16	4⅛	9¼
510	24¾	30½	....	1/16	5¼	....
515	17½	....	....	1/16	6½	....
520	14	22⅜	....	1/16	7⅛	....
525	9¾	18	29¼	1/16	8½	....
530	4⅞	15⅝	22¼	1/16	9⅞	16⅞
535	1/16	13	21¾	1/16	12½	17¼
540	1/16	9¾	....	5¼	14½	....
545	1/16	8½	....	9½	16⅜	....
550	1/16	6	....	15	....	....
555	....	4¼	....	....	....	....
560	....	2 15/16	7⅞	....	....	....
565	....	1 15/16	6	....	....	....
570	....	1 5/16	4⅞	....	....	....
575	....	13/16	3⅞	....	....	....
580	....	⅝	....	44½	43	....
585	....	½	....	....	....	....
590	....	⅜	....	....	....	....
595	....	3/16	....	....	....	....

Total call volume 26,865 Total call open int. 77,008
Total put volume 16,395 Total put open int. 82,706
The index: High 536.51; Low 529.85; Close 534.89, +1.31

FUTURES

	Open	High	Low	Settle	Chg	Lifetime High	Lifetime Low	Open Interest
S&P 500 INDEX (CME) 500 times index								
Dec	319.80	320.80	315.80	319.30	+ 1.25	379.50	295.60	140,591
Mr91	322.40	323.50	318.55	321.90	+ 1.25	384.00	298.00	14,001
June	326.30	326.30	321.50	324.75	+ 1.10	386.00	300.90	1,367
Est vol 53,236; vol Thur 47,200; open int 155,986, −3,014.								
Indx prelim High 318.80; Low 314.99; Close 317.12 +.10								
NYSE COMPOSITE INDEX (NYFE) 500 times index								
Dec	174.45	174.90	172.15	174.20	+ .55	206.50	161.25	4,258
Mr91	175.85	175.95	173.50	175.00	+ .55	183.00	163.85	348
Est vol 6,039; vol Thur 6,144; open int 4,658, −15.								
The index: High 174.11; Low 172.36; Close 173.30 +.18								
MAJOR MKT INDEX (CBT) $250 times index								
Nov	536.00	537.40	529.70	534.80	+ 1.85	544.25	491.25	3,525
Dec	537.50	539.75	532.00	537.75	+ 2.15	543.30	493.25	4,617
Ja91	536.30	539.75	536.30	539.75	+ 2.25	545.25	508.00	152
Est vol 7,000; vol Thur 6,084; open int 8,294, +247.								
The index: High 536.51; Low 529.85; Close 534.89 +1.31								

—OTHER INDEX FUTURES—

Settlement price of selected contract. Volume and open interest of all contract months.

KC Mini Value Line (KC)—100 times Index
Dec 229.90 +.40; Est. vol. 30; Open int. 156
KC Value Line Index (KC)—500 times Index
Dec 230.05 +.55; Est. vol. 150; Open int. 1,263
The index: High 229.80; Low 228.36; Close 229.11 +.03
CRB Index (NYFE)—250 times Index
Dec 225.85 +.70; Est. vol. 218; Open int. 1,493
The index: High 226.33; Low 224.20; Close 226.22 +1.28
NIKKEI 225 Stock Average (CME)—$5 times NSA
Dec 23650.00 +1.85; Est. vol. 725; Open int. 3,751
The index: High 23455.41; Low 23874.39; Close 23171.63 − 315.85

CBT—Chicago Board of Trade. CME—Chicago Mercantile Exchange. KC—Kansas City Board of Trade. NYFE—New York Futures Exchange, a unit of the New York Stock Exchange.

FUTURES OPTIONS

S&P 500 STOCK INDEX (CME) $500 times premium

Strike Price	Calls—Settle Nov-c	Calls—Settle Dec-c	Calls—Settle Mr-c	Puts—Settle Nov-p	Puts—Settle Dec-p	Puts—Settle Mar-p
310	9.30	13.35	23.50	0.00	4.15	11.85
315	4.30	9.80	20.35	0.00	5.50	13.55
320	0.00	6.70	17.20	0.70	7.40	15.35
325	0.00	4.25	14.00	5.70	9.90	17.00
330	0.00	2.45	11.00	10.70	13.05	18.90
335	0.00	1.35	8.45	....	16.95	21.25

Est. vol. 13,095; Thur vol. 1,856 calls; 3,002 puts
Open interest Thur; 42,738 calls; 44,177 puts

—OTHER INDEX FUTURES OPTIONS—

NYSE COMPOSITE INDEX (NYFE) $500 times premium

Strike Price	Calls—Settle Nov-c	Calls—Settle Dec-c	Calls—Settle Mar-c	Puts—Settle Nov-p	Puts—Settle Dec-p	Puts—Settle Mar-p
174	.05	3.70	6.40	0.00	3.70	5.35

Est. vol. 308, Thur vol. 45 calls, 47 puts
Open interest Thur 1,044 calls, 1,056 puts

NIKKEI 225 STOCK AVERAGE (CME) $5 times NSA

Strike Price	Calls—Settle Nov-c	Calls—Settle Dec-c	Calls—Settle Mar-c	Puts—Settle Nov-p	Puts—Settle Dec-p	Puts—Settle Mar-p
23500	150	1010	1975	0.00	8.50	....

Est. vol. 138, Thur vol. 144 calls, 0 puts
Open interest Thur 972 calls, 2,157 puts
CBT—Chicago Board of Trade. CME—Chicago Mercantile Exchange. NYFE—New York Futures Exchange, a unit of the New York Stock Exchange.

Source: *The Wall Street Journal,* Monday, November 19, 1990

**Figure 5-4   Risk/Reward Diagrams of Vertical Bull Call Spreads
December 1990 S&P 500 Futures Options at Expiration**

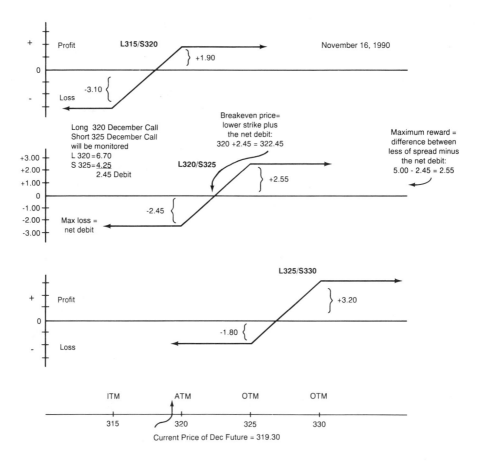

and selling two 325 December S&P 500 calls will be monitored in this case study. The price of the December future is 319.30. Thus, this spread involves buying the closest out-of-the-money calls and selling calls one strike higher. This is a reasonable starting position for a bullish options trader. Although the technical expectation is that the price of the December S&P futures will move substantially higher, a follow-up strategy of lifting the losing leg should be easy in these liquid options.

Initial Position
Long two 320 Dec calls at 6.70 x 2   =   –13.40
Short two 325 Dec calls at 4.25 x 2   =   8.50
Debit   =   –4.90

4.90 pts. x 500 $US / 1.00 pt. = 2,450 $US
(cost of initial position before commissions)

Traders with a bias to the more traditional (and liquid) equity options would achieve parallel results using vertical bull call spreads in the S&P 100 Index (OEX) options traded on the Chicago Board Options Exchange (CBOE) or Major Market Index (MMI) options traded on the American Stock Exchange. Options on the Major Market Index futures began trading on the Chicago Board of Trade in October 1991—11 months after this case study.

The Major Market Index (MMI) is highly correlated with the Dow Jones Industrial Average. The 20 blue-chip issues that compose the MMI are listed in Table 5-3. The high correlation between the Dow Industrials and the MMI can easily be seen when the two charts are superimposed as in Figure 5-5.

Volatility

Volatility to an options trader is defined as one standard deviation of daily price change in one year. It is expressed as a percent. Volatility is the most subjective variable of the five (futures) or six (stocks) inputs necessary to calculate a theoretical price for an option (see Appendix B). The two forms of volatility that will be addressed in this book are historical and implied.

- *Historical volatility:* Volatility that can be calculated over any number of trading days (e.g., 20, 30, 60, 120, 250, etc.).

- *Implied volatility:* Volatility that the marketplace is imputing into the underlying future, given the current (actual) price of the option.

Figure 5-6 shows both the historical and implied volatilities for the S&P 500 Index and its options. The 21 percent implied volatility that existed on November 16 suggests that the S&P can be expected to remain within a range

Table 5-3   Major Market Index Securities as of November 13, 1990

Company Name*	Symbol	Market Value (000's$)	Shares Out (000's)	Closing Price ($)	Price as a % of Index
IBM	IBM	64,159,088	572,849	112.00	10.47
MERCK	MRK	32,299,930	390,922	82.63	7.73
PROCTER & GAMBLE	PG	28,093,101	346,294	81.13	7.59
3M	MMM	17,646,615	221,970	79.50	7.44
CHEVRON	CHV	24,482,576	353,539	69.25	6.48
JOHNSON & JOHNSON	JNJ	22,071,055	333,148	66.25	6.20
MOBIL	MOB	23,864,309	406,201	58.75	5.49
GENERAL ELECTRIC	GE	49,318,244	888,617	55.50	5.19
EXXON	XON	62,353,450	1,247,069	50.00	4.68
INTERNATIONAL PAPER	IP	5,338,714	109,232	48.88	4.57
PHILIP MORRIS	MO	44,833,788	924,408	48.50	4.54
COCA COLA	KO	30,040,515	667,567	45.00	4.21
DOW CHEMICAL	DOW	11,595,982	269,674	43.00	4.02
EASTMAN KODAK	EK	13,424,698	324,464	41.38	3.87
GENERAL MOTORS	GM	23,476,869	601,971	39.00	3.65
DU PONT	DD	23,389,153	675,499	34.63	3.24
AT&T	T	36,075,212	1,089,063	33.13	3.10
USX	X	8,095,456	254,975	31.75	2.97
SEARS ROEBUCK	S	9,088,864	342,976	26.50	2.48
AMERICAN EXPRESS	AXP	10,402,898	462,351	22.50	2.10

*Listing is ranked by price of stock

MMI Formula

Major Market Index = Sum of component stock prices divided by divisor
Divisor is currently 2.00742

MMI Divisor Adjustments

Effective Date of Change	New Divisor
May 11, 1990 (current)	2.00742
Jan 22, 1990	2.08185
Nov 21, 1989	2.23510
Nov 20, 1989	2.29441
Oct 11, 1989	2.41744
May 11, 1989	2.66280
Mar 29, 1989	2.76558
May 26, 1988	2.85813
Jan 19, 1988	3.11985
Oct 20, 1987	3.12165

Figure 5-5   MMI Futures Versus DJIA

Major Market Index futures trade on the Chicago
Board of Trade. Options on the index trade on
the American Stock Exchange

Figure 5-6   S&P 500 Volatility Charts

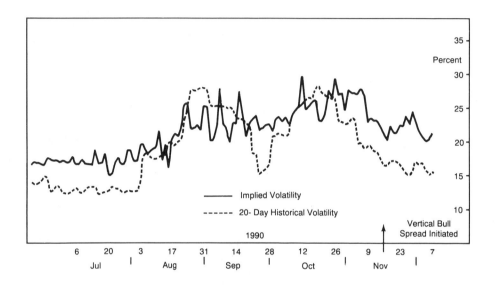

of 21 percent plus or minus * its current price at the end of a year with about 67 percent confidence; or that prices will remain within a two standard deviation range (plus or minus 42 percent) with 95 percent confidence.

The 21 percent implied volatility seems reasonable with respect to the most recent band of 20 to 28 percent in which implied volatility has been moving. When the implied volatility of 21 percent is compared to the historical 20-day volatility of 16 1/2 percent, the options appear overpriced. The marketplace obviously does not expect the S&P 500 Index to be as quiet as it has been.

Volatility does not have a major impact for directionally biased vertical spreaders. Therefore the 21 percent implied volatility reading for the at-the-money S&P 500 futures options does not force a trader into a particular spread strictly for volatility reasons. Additional insights into volatility con-

---

* Most theoretical pricing models assume that price *changes* are normally distributed. This results in a log-normal distribution for price at expiration. Thus, a representative model will actually predict slightly higher prices at expiration than simply plus or minus 21 percent of the current price.

Figure 5-7   Major Market Index Options

A.

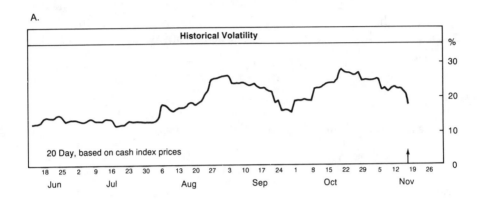

B.

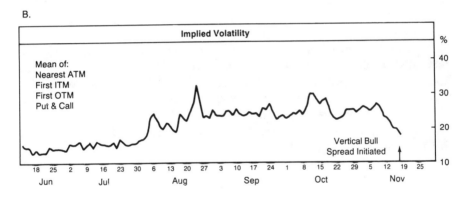

Table 5-4   Implied Volatility Data Points, Major Market Index

09/24/90	27.11	10/08/90	23.70	10/22/90	22.37	11/05/90	24.80
09/25/90	24.70	10/09/90	25.78	10/23/90	22.83	11/06/90	25.54
09/26/90	22.50	10/10/90	29.92	10/24/90	23.54	11/07/90	27.24
09/27/90	23.45	10/11/90	29.95	10/25/90	25.36	11/08/90	26.13
09/28/90	23.76	10/12/90	28.24	10/26/90	25.37	11/09/90	23.34
10/01/90	22.67	10/15/90	26.85	10/29/90	25.52	11/12/90	22.78
10/02/90	23.54	10/16/90	28.06	10/30/90	24.46	11/13/90	21.70
10/03/90	24.43	10/17/90	28.64	10/31/90	25.46	11/14/90	19.77
10/04/90	24.17	10/18/90	25.17	11/01/90	26.24	11/15/90	19.91
10/05/90	25.14	10/19/90	22.89	11/02/90	25.83	11/16/90	17.79

siderations can be found in Figure 9-2 and in Chapter Fifteen—Volatility Forecasting.

Figures 5-7A&B and the implied volatility figures in Table 5-4 show that options on the Major Market Index are trading very close to the 20-day historical volatility of 18 percent. The implied volatility on November 16 was 17.79 percent.

Upside Breakout: Remove One-Half of Losing Leg

Friday, November 30, 1990

An upside breakout from the larger Head & Shoulders Bottom on the Dec S&P 500 chart occurred on Friday, November 30 (Figure 5-8). Volume expanded to 72,396 contracts, confirming the validity of the breakout. The minimum upside measuring objective is 354.25.

Aggressive traders should remove one-half of the losing leg of the vertical spreads. This entails buying back (covering) 50 percent of the call options that were previously sold short. The long 320 versus short 325 Dec S&P 500 call spread will continue to be used as the example.

If a pullback (prices decline) to the larger neckline occurs, the remaining (one-half) short call position should be covered. This would leave the trader in the most bullish options condition—long calls. Note that the strategy matrix in Chapter Two states that the ideal technical situation for a long call position is "en route to price pattern measuring objective after pullback has occurred."

Option Prices for Close November 30

S&P 500 STOCK INDEX (CME) $500 times premium

Strike Price	Calls—Settle			Puts—Settle		
	Dec-c	Jan-c	Mr-c	Dec-p	Jan-p	Mar-p
315	11.40	17.55	22.80	2.40	5.95	11.30
320	7.75	14.00	19.55	3.70	7.35	13.00
325	4.75	10.60	16.25	5.70	8.90	14.55
330	2.50	7.70	13.25	8.40	....	16.40
335	1.25	5.30	10.65	12.15	....	18.70
340	.60	3.40	8.40	16.50	....	21.30

Est. vol. 7,235; Thur vol. 1,063 calls; 2,401 puts
Open interest Thur ; 41,381 calls; 51,120 puts

Dec futures = 324.05

Original Position
Vertical bull call spread

Long two 320 Dec calls at 6.70 x 2	=	−13.40
Short two 325 Dec calls at 4.25 x 2	=	8.50
Debit	=	−4.90

Figure 5-8   Upside Breakout from Larger H&S Bottom
Remove One-Half of Losing Leg

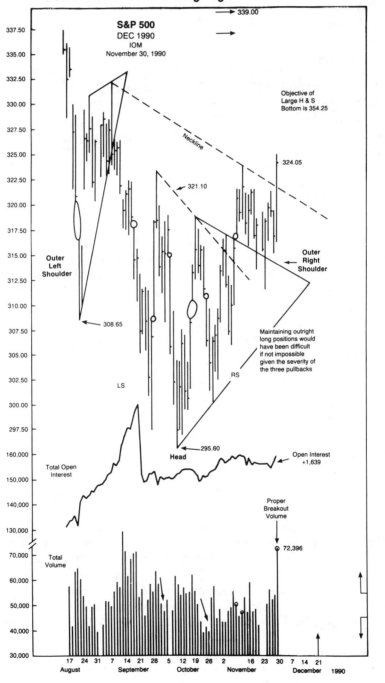

Follow-up
Lift one-half of losing leg
Buy one 325 Dec call at 4.75
(for a loss of 4.25 – 4.75 = –0.50)

Present Position
Long two 320 Dec calls
Open trade profit = (7.75 – 6.70) x 2 = 1.05 x 2 = 2.10
Short one 325 Dec call
Open trade loss = 4.25 – 4.75 = –0.50

Risk/Reward Parameters of New Position

After every modification of an options strategy, the trader must be aware of
the new profit or loss characteristics. A simple method of constructing the
risk/reward graph involves creating a profit/loss table as shown in Table
5-5. Using a spreadsheet format, a trader lists the individual present positions and the costs involved in getting there in Column A. Possible values
at expiration (both above and below the spread strike prices) head the
remaining columns. Each cell entry is calculated and the resulting outcome
is tabulated in the bottom row.

Graph paper of similar scale to the chart of the underlying should be
used to plot the possible outcomes as shown in Figure 5-9. It is obvious that
this new position of long more calls than short is much more aggressively
bullish than the original position. Above the upper 325 strike, the options
position acts (at expiration) like a long S&P 500 futures contract.

Important World Stock Index Charts as of Friday, December 14, 1990

Confirmation of the S&P 500 upside breakout from the Complex H&S
Bottom occurred on the Dow Jones Industrial Average on December 14—
also on increased turnover. This can be observed in Figure 5-10.

The December S&P chart (Figure 5-11) exhibits the possibility that a
Falling Wedge pattern is developing. This is a bullish pattern composed of
four reversals of the minor price trend similar to a Symmetrical Triangle (see
Chapter Eight). Both boundary lines of a Falling Wedge slope downward.
A close above the upper boundary line activates a measuring objective of a
new price high above reversal point 1.

Interesting technical situations existed on many of the world's equity
index charts. Specifically:

Table 5-5   Tabular Risk/Reward of Follow-up Position

Column A	B	C	D	E	F
	Possible Expiration Prices				
	315	**320**	**325**	**330**	**335**
Value of long two 320 calls	0	0	+10.00	+20.00	+30.00
Value of short one 325 call	0	0	0	−5.00	−10.00
Debit of original two-lot spread	−4.90	−4.90	−4.90	−4.90	−4.90
Follow-up of lifting one-half of losing leg	−0.50	−0.50	−0.50	−0.50	−0.50
Outcome to trader	−5.40	−5.40	+4.60	+9.60	+14.60

Figure 5-9   Graphic Risk/Reward Diagram of Follow-up Position

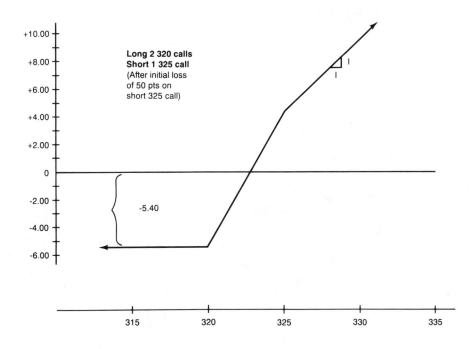

1. Dow Jones Industrial Average (2593.81)—Figure 5-10

    A. Complex Head & Shoulders Bottom
    B. Minimum upside measuring objective = 2850

2. S&P 500 December future (327.20)—Figure 5-11

    A. Complex Head & Shoulders Bottom
    B. Minimum upside measuring objective = 354.25
    C. Possible Bullish Falling Wedge
        i.   Upside breakout = close above 330.50
        ii. Volume parameters:
             60,000+ = high
             52,000– = low
        iii. If activated, objective = 335.00+

3. S&P 100 Cash Index OEX (307.56)—Figure 5-12

    A. Complex Head & Shoulders Bottom
    B. Minimum upside measuring objective = 335.00

4. Nikkei 225 Candle Chart (24,349.50)—Figure 5-13

    A. Possible Head & Shoulders Bottom
    B. Neckline = 24,850

5. Hang Seng Index (3125.69)—Figure 5-14

    A. Possible Complex Head & Shoulders Bottom
    B. Inner H&S Bottom activated
        i.   Breakout was 3055
        ii. Minimum measuring objective = 3380

6. European Stock Markets—Bottoming Tendencies—Figure 5-15

    A. London FTSE–100 (2168.4)
    B. Frankfurt DAX (1522.40)
    C. Paris CAC–40 (1635.52)

7. International Business Machines Common Stock (111 1/4)—Figure 5-16

    A. Possible Rare H&S Bottom Continuation Pattern
        i.   Neckline = 114 1/4
        ii. High volume = 1.6 million+ shares
        iii. If activated, objective = 119 3/8
    B. Pattern Gap at 112 7/8 should be filled
    C. Large Double Bottom
        i.   Traditional objective = 124 3/8
        ii. Support = 110 3/8

Figure 5-10   Complex Head & Shoulders Bottom

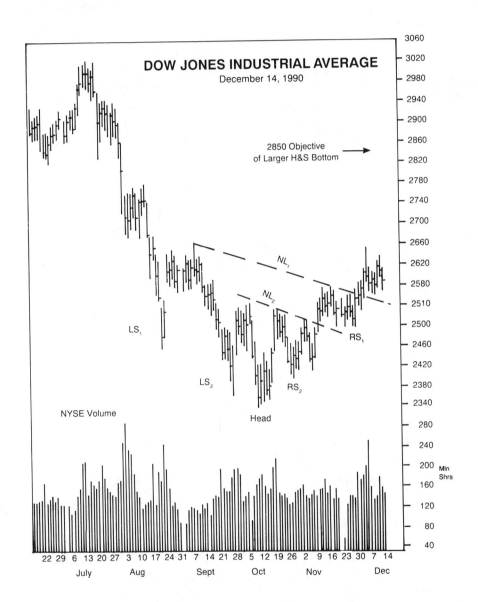

Figure 5-11   Complex Head & Shoulders Bottom

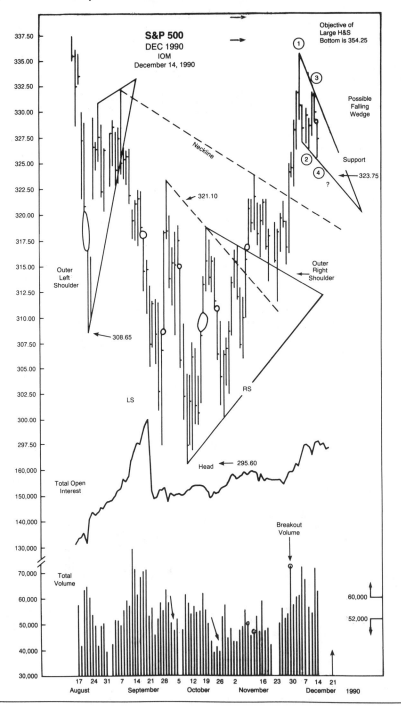

Figure 5-12   Complex Head & Shoulders Bottom

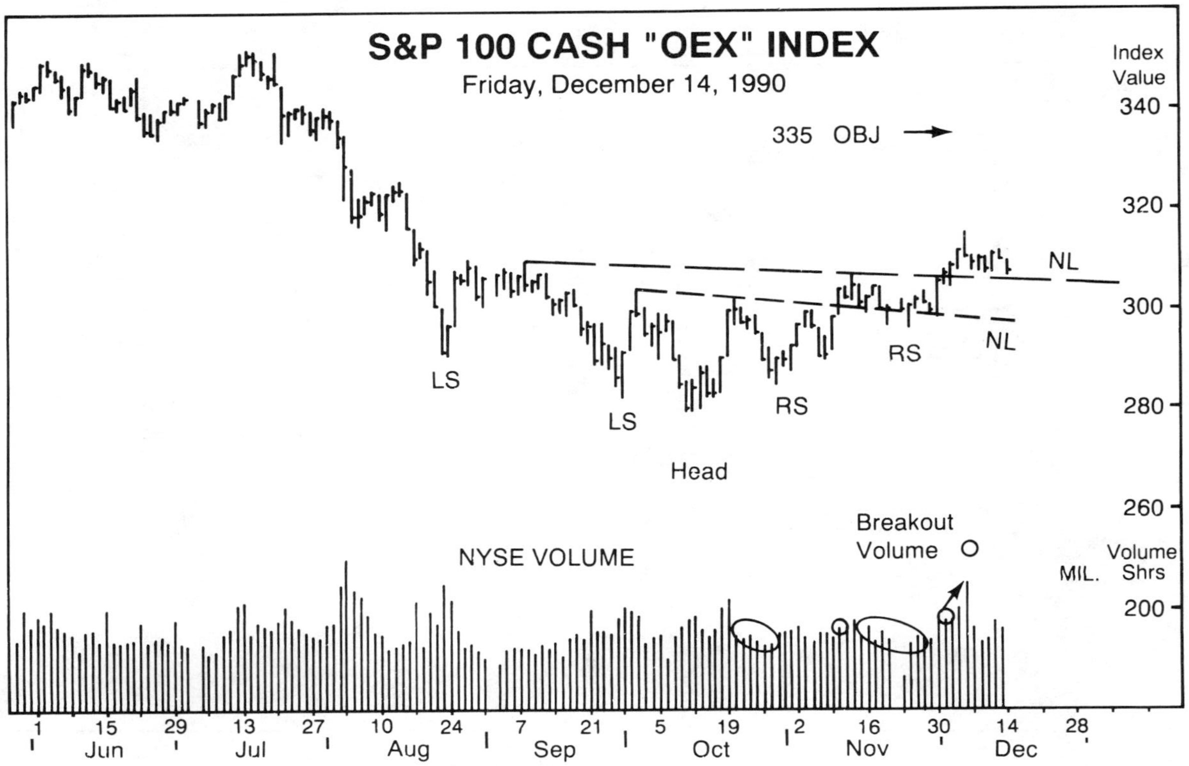

S&P 100 CASH "OEX" INDEX
Friday, December 14, 1990

335 OBJ →

Index Value

340

320

300

280

260

Volume Shrs
MIL.

200

NL

NL

RS

RS

LS

LS

LS

Head

NYSE VOLUME

Breakout Volume O

Jun 15 29 Jul 13 27 Aug 10 24 Sep 7 21 Oct 5 19 Nov 2 16 30 Dec 14 28

Figure 5-13   Possible Head & Shoulders Bottom

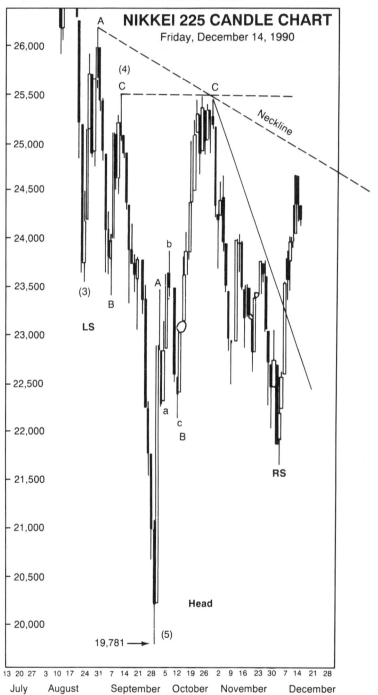

Figure 5-14   Possible Complex Head & Shoulders Bottom

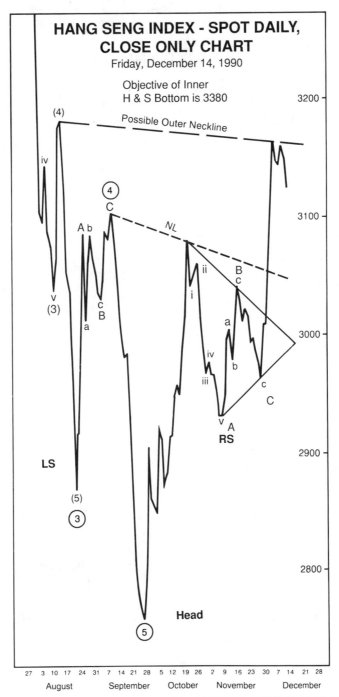

HANG SENG INDEX - SPOT DAILY,
CLOSE ONLY CHART
Friday, December 14, 1990

Objective of Inner
H & S Bottom is 3380

Figure 5-15   Bottoming Tendencies, Friday December 14, 1990

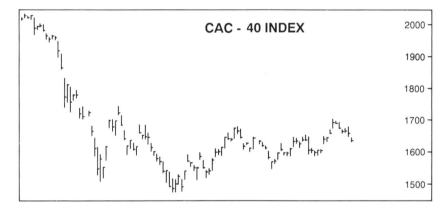

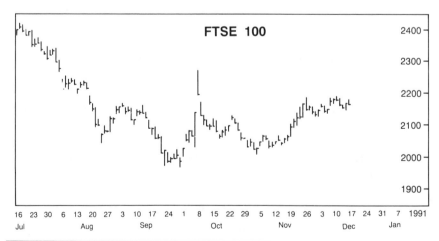

Figure 5-16   Double Bottom

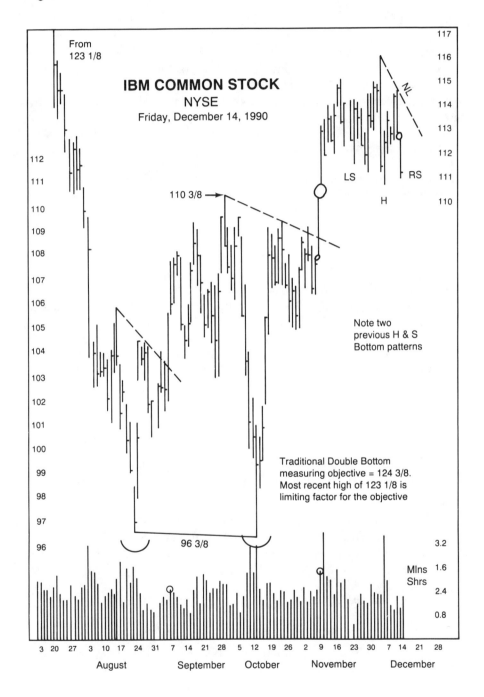

IBM COMMON STOCK
NYSE
Friday, December 14, 1990

Week Prior to Expiration of December S&P Options

The S&P chart in Figure 5-17 is plotted through the opening on Friday, December 21. The special opening quotation on the third Friday of the contract month is the cash settlement price for the S&P 500 options. But the four prior daily price postings made for an interesting week of trading. The sequence of events is listed below. Technical comments concerning several other important financial instruments are also stated, although their charts are not specifically shown.

Monday, December 17

A lower low (than Friday) occurred on Monday in the Dow Industrials, the S&P 500 futures (both December and March) and IBM. The major technical question to be answered: Is the bullish Falling Wedge price pattern on the S&P chart still possible? The answer is yes.

Tuesday, December 18

The U.S. stock market opened firmer on Tuesday morning, December 18. In-the-money January 110 IBM calls could have easily been purchased at 4 7/8 (IBM last = 112 3/8). The Dow Industrials were trading +11.00 in the early afternoon; the December S&P 500 futures were +0.80, trading at 327.55. The December 330 S&P 500 calls could have been purchased at 1.05.

With approximately one hour remaining to trade in the S&P futures (2:15 CST), the Fed lowered the discount rate. The S&P 500 futures rallied to up 5.00, the Dow to up 36 and IBM to up 2.

Tuesday evening

1. U.S. T-bond futures gap opened 27 ticks higher (at 5:00 p.m. CST) in the Tuesday evening session that officially began Wednesday's trade.

2. The Hang Seng Index sold off when the Hong Kong & Shanghai Banking Corporation reincorporated under a U.K. holding company. This created a possible outer right shoulder of a Complex H&S Bottom on the chart.

Wednesday, December 19

1. In trade in Japan on Wednesday:

    •   A gap opening to the upside (between 24,424.02 and 24,473.32) occurred on the Nikkei 225; this was a Breakaway Gap.

Figure 5-17   December Expiration

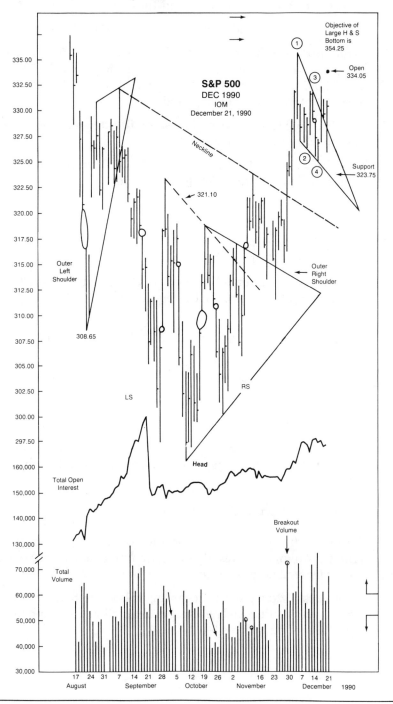

- Volume for the first section was estimated at 620 million shares—up from 382.1 million shares on Tuesday.

- The Nikkei 225 traded and closed (24,876.78) above its neckline.

2. Actual S&P 500 futures volume for Tuesday was 60,571. Volume parameters at the time were: 60,000+ for the high and 52,000– for the low. Thus, the turnover was high enough to validate the upside breakout of the bullish Falling Wedge.

3. Total S&P 500 futures open interest for Tuesday rose 956 contracts; this too was a bullish technical sign.

4. A pullback occurred in early trade in the S&P futures. This brought quotes back to the Falling Wedge breakout.

Thursday, December 20

1. Share prices gap opened lower in the U.S. after the resignation of Soviet Foreign Minister Shevardnadze.

2. After a major U.S. bank lowered its prime lending rate from 10 percent to 9 1/2 percent, the U.S. equity markets rallied to close the gaps.

3. Is the Falling Wedge pattern on the S&P, Dow Industrials and IBM charts still viable?

- December S&P 500—Yes.

- March S&P 500—Lower line needs to be redrawn.

- Dow Industrials—Yes.

- IBM—Closed at 113 3/4—out the upside of a Falling Wedge on Thursday. Volume was 1.9 million shares (high). The objective is 116+.

Friday, December 21—Options Expiration Day

1. An unusually strong opening in the S&P 500 Index occurred on Friday morning. This resulted in a final settlement price of 334.05 for the December future (seen as a dot in Figure 5-17).

2. An interesting observation regarding this expiration was made in *Barron's* weekly financial newspaper. Expiration prices and the comments are found in Table 5-6.

OUTCOME OF DECEMBER OPTIONS POSITIONS
AND CASE STUDY 1

The technical situation that existed on the December S&P 500 futures chart on the open December 21 is shown in Figure 5-17. The pullback toward the breakout of the larger H&S Bottom did not completely reach the neckline. Thus, a low-risk technical situation did not occur so the remaining one-half of the losing leg of the options spread could be lifted. Figure 5-17 also shows that the minimum upside measuring objectives of the inner and outer H&S Bottoms have not yet been achieved. Thus, the March S&P 500 futures chart should be examined for confirmation of a continued bullish view. This will be undertaken in Case Study 2.

The expiring December option position can be thought of as long one vertical bull call spread and additionally long one call option. The expiration prices were:

320 calls expired at 14.05
325 calls expired at 9.05

Note that the spread is at its maximuum differential of 5.00; this is equal to the distance between the legs of the spread.

The S&P 500 futures are cash settled (no physical delivery), and the options expire along with the futures; thus, the options can also be considered cash settled. The exchange simply marks the positions to the market. Following is a summary of the overall December options position and Case Study 1.

Initial cost of one vertical spread	=	−2.45	
Spread at expiration	=	+5.00	
Credit	=		+2.55
Initial cost of one long 320 call	=	−6.70	
Long 320 call at expiration	=	+14.05	
Credit	=		+7.35
Loss on one short 325 call	=		−0.50
(detailed on page 44)			+9.40

+9.40 pts x 500 $US/per point = 4,700 $US
(profit before commissions)

Table 5-6 Final December S&P 500 Options Settlements and a Comment from *Barron's*, December 24, 1990

Chicago Mercantile Exchange

CAB represents a cabinet trade or when an investor is getting out of a position.

S&P 500

S&P CALL

Month	Strike	Vol	Open Int	Week's High	Week's Low	Sett	Pt Chg	Future Sett
DEC 90	275			----	----	59.05	+ 685	334.05
DEC 90	280		1	----	----	54.05	+ 685	334.05
DEC 90	285			----	----	49.05	+ 685	334.05
DEC 90	290		2	----	----	44.05	+ 685	334.05
DEC 90	295		10	----	----	39.05	+ 685	334.05
DEC 90	300	1125	581	30.00	----	34.05	+ 680	334.05
DEC 90	305	3	1622	----	----	29.05	+ 675	334.05
DEC 90	310	1	816	----	----	24.05	+ 665	334.05
DEC 90	315	171	1241	15.90	----	19.05	+ 650	334.05
DEC 90	320	4465	3698	11.00	----	14.05	+ 610	334.05
DEC 90	325	427	1719	6.20	----	9.05	+ 495	334.05
DEC 90	330	2193	2114	2.80	----	4.05	+ 250	334.05
DEC 90	335	1440	2700	.70	CAB	CAB	– 45	334.05
DEC 90	340	398	2114	.15	CAB	CAB	– 10	334.05
DEC 90	345	190	1171	.05	CAB	CAB		334.05
DEC 90	350	1	1385	CAB	CAB	CAB		334.05
DEC 90	355		3390	----	----	CAB		334.05
DEC 90	360		3520	----	----	CAB		334.05
DEC 90	365		610	----	----	CAB		334.05
DEC 90	370		480	----	----	CAB		334.05
DEC 90	375		249	----	----	CAB		334.05
DEC 90	380		746	----	----	CAB		334.05
DEC 90	385		261	----	----	CAB		334.05
DEC 90	390		425	----	----	CAB		334.05
DEC 90	395		317	----	----	CAB		334.05
DEC 90	400		337	----	----	CAB		334.05
DEC 90	410		40	----	----	CAB		334.05
JAN 91	305		76	----	----	30.85	+ 415	334.75
JAN 91	310	1	74	24.70	----	26.20	+ 380	334.75
JAN 91	315		29	----	----	21.75	+ 350	334.75
JAN 91	320	37	381	16.80	12.75	17.35	+ 295	334.75
JAN 91	325	13	110	12.90	9.60	13.25	+ 235	334.75
JAN 91	330	443	553	9.00	6.60	9.65	+ 185	334.75
JAN 91	335	152	220	6.40	4.00	6.35	+ 110	334.75
JAN 91	340	2282	2469	4.20	2.50	3.90	+ 65	334.75
JAN 91	345	71	107	2.40	1.25	2.00	+ 15	334.75
JAN 91	350	214	263	1.10	.90	.85	– 15	334.75
JAN 91	355	1	9	.55	.45	.40	– 10	334.75
JAN 91	360	207	206	.40	.30	.30		334.75
FEB 91	305		40	----	----	33.15	+ 370	334.75
FEB 91	325		52	----	----	16.95	+ 225	334.75
FEB 91	335	2	130	9.00	----	10.20	+ 155	334.75
FEB 91	340		252	7.10	6.20	7.60	+ 120	334.75
FEB 91	345	27	27	4.60	----	5.15	+ 75	334.75
FEB 91	350	4	149	3.40	2.75	3.40	+ 55	334.75
MAR 91	270		1	----	----	66.00	+ 470	334.75
MAR 91	285		75	----	----	52.25	+ 415	334.75
MAR 91	295	1	3	39.40	----	43.75	+ 410	334.75
MAR 91	300	2084	837	38.80	33.70	39.50	+ 395	334.75
MAR 91	305		164	34.00	----	35.25	+ 370	334.75
MAR 91	310	2	561	30.00	----	31.10	+ 340	334.75
MAR 91	315	12	428	25.90	----	27.35	+ 330	334.75
MAR 91	320	155	412	22.10	----	23.25	+ 270	334.75
MAR 91	325	90	313	19.20	16.00	19.55	+ 225	334.75
MAR 91	330	197	599	15.65	13.30	16.10	+ 185	334.75
MAR 91	335	342	5136	12.75	10.70	12.90	+ 145	334.75
MAR 91	340	421	4771	10.10	7.80	10.05	+ 110	334.75
MAR 91	345	60	318	7.30	----	7.55	+ 80	334.75
MAR 91	350	107	723	5.00	----	5.35	+ 45	334.75
MAR 91	355	104	131	3.60	----	3.60	+ 15	334.75
MAR 91	360	2	290	2.50	----	2.35	+ 5	334.75
MAR 91	370	50	99	1.00	----	.80	– 5	334.75
MAR 91	380		50	.35	----	.25		334.75
MAR 91	390		62	----	----	.10		334.75
JUN 91	320		30	----	----	31.40	+ 215	337.70
JUN 91	330		36	23.40	----	24.20	+ 90	337.70
JUN 91	340	4	96	17.00	16.30	18.05	+ 55	337.70
JUN 91	350	21	250	12.00	----	12.30	+ 35	337.70
JUN 91	360	190	523	8.00	7.80	8.40	+ 40	337.70
JUN 91	370		10	----	----	5.75	+ 25	337.70
JUN 91	380	13	66	3.20	----	3.15	+ 15	337.70
JUN 91	390		5	----	----	2.00	+ 10	337.70
JUN 91	400		160	----	----	1.45	+ 5	337.70

AN NYSE specialist suggests to this column that expiration Fridays are a trading opportunity. Arbitrageurs place orders to buy or sell that can add up on one side of the market; the specialist viewed it as his profitable duty to help out the arbs.

It's a game the public can play. Imbalance indications resulting from orders placed before last Friday's opening, relating to expiration of some derivative products at values determined by the opening, began to show on the news tape at 9 a.m., and were all on the buy side. Generally the indications were of 150,000 shares to buy, but for **Wal-Mart**, **Exxon** and **AT&T**, the figure exceeded 500,000 shares. With buy-side imbalances, a trader or investor who believes Thursday's close on a stock is a full-value price stands a chance of profiting nicely by placing an order with a higher price limit for such a Friday opening. Here's how it would have worked last Friday morning for some of the stocks involved in arb orders.

	Thurs. Close	Fri. Open	High
Exxon	50⅜	51	51
AT&T	30⅜	31⅜	31⅜
Wal-Mart	31	31⅜	31⅞
BellSouth	54¾	56¼	56¼
AIG	79⅝	81	81
USWest	39¼	40½	40½
Sears	25¾	26½	26½
Lilly	74¼	75	75
Disney	100⅜	101¾	101¾
Boeing	45⅞	46⅝	46⅝
P&G	86½	87¼	87¼

It's interesting to note the number of arbitrage orders the floor was able to fill at the day's highs. ■

Case Study 2: March 1991 S&P 500 Options

The minimum upside measuring objective on the March S&P 500 futures chart from Figure 5-18 is 355.00. This is derived from the largest of the Head & Shoulders Bottom formations. Because a Falling Wedge pattern has been activated, a technician would assume the pullback toward the breakout from the Head & Shoulders Bottom is finished. This technical situation dictates the most aggressive options posture—long calls.

The next question is which calls should be purchased? The implied volatility declines as the call options are further out-of-the-money (see Table 5-7). But the percentage return based on the current cost versus expected return declines as further out-of-the-money options are analyzed. The assumption is made that the March future is trading exactly at 355.00 (the H&S Bottom objective) at expiration. The percentage returns are shown in Table 5-8.

The simplistic analysis in Table 5-8 does not annualize the returns or take into consideration interest costs. But it does show that trying to buy the lower cost out-of-the-money 350 strike calls is the worst strategy. As usual, it takes money to make money!

For the purpose of this case study, the position of long two at-the-money March 335 call options will be monitored. The cost of each of these options as of the close Friday, December 21 is 12.90.

Present Position
Long two 335 Mar calls at 12.90 x 2 = 25.80
25.80 x 500 $US = 12,900 $US (cost of initial position before commisions)

Fail-Safe Trendline in Jeopardy

Friday, January 4, 1991

The Dow Jones Industrial Average chart in Figure 5-19 shows that the closing price for trading on January 4 was just above the last possible support line. The Dow chart looks stronger than the chart of the March S&P 500. Figure 5-20 shows that the last fail-safe trendline on the S&P chart has already been violated by a close below it on Friday.

The large Complex Head & Shoulders Bottom has not been destroyed on the various equity charts, but prudent trading typically forces a technician to the sidelines when the fail-safe trendline is penetrated. This is

Figure 5-18 March S&P 500 Futures Chart at Expiration of December Options

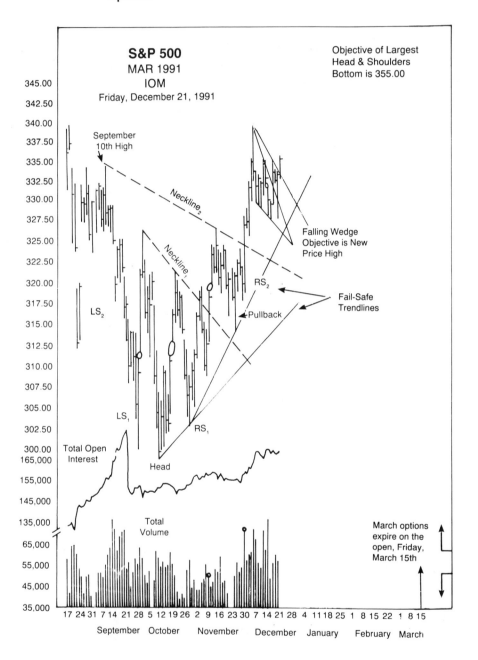

Table 5-7   March 1991 S&P 500 Options

Futures Price	Estimated Volatility	Interest Rate	Start Date	Expiration Date
334.8	20.5%	6.1%	12-21-1990	03-14-1991

	Calls			Puts		
Strike Price	Theoretical Premium	Actual Premium	Implied Volatility	Theoretical Premium	Actual Premium	Implied Volatility
360.0	4.4			29.3		
355.0	5.6			25.6		
350.0	7.0	5.4	17.7%	22.0	20.4	17.0%
345.0	8.6	7.8	19.1%	18.7	17.7	19.0%
340.0	10.5	10.1	19.9%	15.7	15.3	20.0%
335.0	12.8	12.9	20.5%	13.0	13.2	20.7%
330.0	15.3	16.1	21.6%	10.6	11.5	21.9%
325.0	18.1	19.6	23.2%	8.4	10.0	23.0%
320.0	21.2			6.6		
315.0	24.6			5.1		
310.0	28.2			3.8		
305.0	32.1			2.8		

Note: All prices have been rounded to one decimal place
Source: Options & Alternatives , Chicago Mercantile Exchange

Table 5-8   March 1991 S&P 500 Call Analysis

Strike	Cost 21 Dec 1990	Option Value with Future at 355	Gain Loss ±	Percent Return
335	12.90	20.00	+7.10	7.10/12.90 = 55%
340	10.05	15.00	+4.95	4.95/10.05 = 49.3%
345	7.55	10.00	+2.45	2.45/7.55 = 32.5%
350	5.35	5.00	−0.35	Negative

especially true with outright long or short positions that contain unlimited risk.

The present position of long call options does contain some staying power. The position will be liquidated to a 50 percent bullish status if the Dow closes below its fail-safe trendline on Monday, January 7.

If overhead resistance at 327.25 on the March S&P chart is violated by a close above it, the long side of the equity market will again look promising. Assuming the price low of the head has not been taken out, the Head & Shoulders Bottom will remain the viable price pattern.

Figure 5-19   Fail-Safe Trendline Being Tested

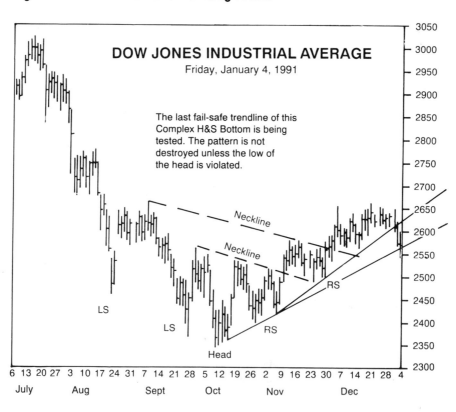

Fail-Safe Trendline Violated: Liquidate One-Half of Long Calls

Monday, January 7, 1991

Both the Dow Jones Industrial Average and the March S&P 500 Index (Figure 5-20) closed lower on Monday, January 7. This dictated that 50 percent of the bullish long call position be liquidated. Option prices are found in Table 5-9.

Original Position
Long two 335 Mar calls at 12.90 x 2 = 25.80

Follow-up: Liquidate one-half of long calls
Sell one Mar 335 call at 4.80
(for a loss of 4.80 – 12.90 = –8.10)

Present Position
Long one Mar 335 call
Open trade loss = –8.10

Redraw the Neckline

Friday, January 18, 1991

The long-term and short-term aspects of the U.S. equity market are easy to see. Figure 5-21 shows the big price rally in the S&P futures on Thursday, January 17 at the start of the Gulf War. This was followed by an Inside Range Day. An Inside Range posting is a minor trend change indicator and implies that at least a minor a selloff is likely. The minimum expectation is that quotes will take out the low of the Inside Range Day.

In addition, a huge Pattern Gap is present below current price levels on all the equity charts. Pattern Gaps are found within trading ranges or congestion areas and are usually quickly filled. On the March S&P 500 chart (Figure 5-21), the gap is located (would be closed) at 319.00. Thus, short term, the S&Ps should try to sell off.

A bullish aspect of the S&P chart is the fact that open interest increased 5,948 contracts on the price rally. Longer term, if the March S&P can close above 340 on volume above 60,000 contracts, a massive Head & Shoulders Bottom will be the operational pattern. *This technical interpretation necessitates redrawing the original neckline of the largest pattern.*

Traders should already be long one March 335 call (from the previous H&S Bottom). To lead off on the new, and much larger, H&S Bottom possibility, vertical bull call spreads would be entered. A conservative trader would wait to see if the Inside Range posting does produce lower prices short term and if the large Pattern Gap is closed.

Looking longer term, the ramifications of the 2660 level on the Dow Jones Industrial Average (Figure 5-22) are obvious to all technicians. A high-volume close above this level would activate an extremely large Head & Shoulders Bottom.

**Figure 5-20   Fail-Safe Trendline Violated
Liquidate One-Half of Long Calls**

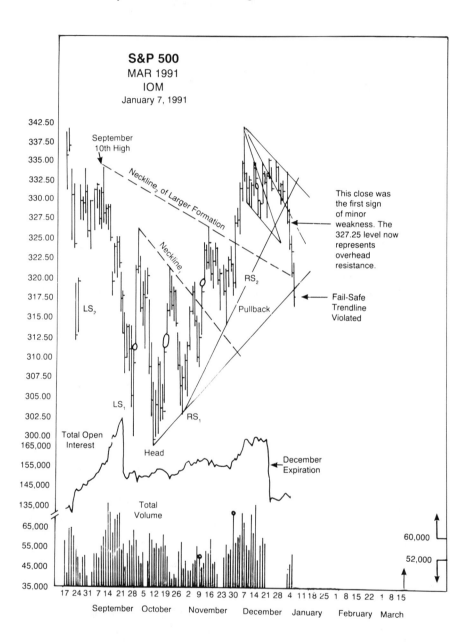

Table 5-9   Index Trading, Monday, January 7, 1991

OPTIONS
Chicago Board

S&P 100 INDEX

Strike Price	Calls–Last			Puts–Last		
	Jan	Feb	Mar	Jan	Feb	Mar
265	....	....	....	1/2	2 3/8	4 1/8
270	....	....	35	11/16	2 3/4	5 1/4
275	25 7/8	28 1/4	....	13/16	3 1/2	6
280	21 1/4	....	....	1 1/4	4 1/4	7 1/4
285	16	....	....	1 3/4	5 3/8	8 1/8
290	10 3/4	16 1/2	21 1/4	2 5/8	7	9 7/8
295	7 1/8	11 3/4	16	4	8 1/2	11 1/4
300	4 1/8	8 1/2	12 3/4	6	10 1/2	13 7/8
305	2 1/8	5 7/8	9 1/2	9	13	15 1/2
310	15/16	3 7/8	7	13	16	18 1/2
315	7/16	2 1/2	5 3/8	17 7/8	19 1/2	20 1/4
320	3/16	1 7/16	3 5/8	22 7/8	23	22 5/8
325	1/8	13/16	2 1/2	26 1/4	26 7/8	....
330	1/16	7/16	1 7/8	28 1/2	....	....
335	1/16	1/4	1	....	....	35

Total call volume 132,761 Total call open int. 297,836
Total put volume 152,883 Total put open int. 361,432
The index: High 302.56; Low 297.06; Close 297.06, −5.50

S&P 500 INDEX

Strike Price	Calls–Last			Puts–Last		
	Jan	Feb	Mar	Jan	Feb	Mar
250	....	....	67 1/2	1/8	13/16	1 1/2
275	....	....	....	....	....	3 1/2
280	....	....	....	....	....	4
285	....	....	....	....	....	4 1/2
290	....	....	....	....	....	5 1/4
295	23 1/2	....	29 1/2	7/8	....	6 1/2
300	20 1/2	24	24 7/8	1 1/2	5	7 5/8
305	13 1/8	....	....	3	6 1/8	8 3/4
310	9 1/4	16 1/4	19 1/4	4 3/4	7 1/4	10 1/2
315	5 3/4	11 3/8	14 1/2	6 7/8	9 3/8	12 1/4
320	3 3/8	7 3/8	12 3/8	10 1/4	9 7/8	14 1/4
325	1 1/2	5 1/4	9	14	13	....
330	7/8	3 3/4	7	18	....	19 1/4
335	1/4	2 3/8	4 5/8	20 1/2	19 5/8	19 1/4
340	3/16	....	3 5/8	27	....	24 1/4
345	1/8	7/8	2	31 1/2	26 3/8	26
350	1/8	3/8	1 1/4	....	31 1/2	32 3/8
355	....	....	3/4	....	....	....
360	....	....	7/16	....	....	....
380	....	....	....	....	....	1/8

Total call volume 32,378 Total call open int. 341,605
Total put volume 23,327 Total put open int. 422,220
The index: High 321.00; Low 315.44; Close 315.44, −5.56

FUTURES

S&P 500 INDEX (CME) 500 times index

	Open	High	Low	Settle	Chg	High	Low	Open Interest
Mar	320.00	321.90	317.20	317.55	− 5.70	384.00	298.00	135,441
June	322.50	324.60	320.00	320.25	− 5.65	386.00	300.90	4,433

Est vol 56,081; vol Fri 47,530; open int 139,901, −1,723.
Indx prelim High 320.97; Low 315.44; Close 315.44 −5.56

NYSE COMPOSITE INDEX (NYFE) 500 times index

Mar	175.00	175.95	173.30	173.65	− 3.00	184.50	163.85	4,558
June	176.35	176.95	174.75	175.00	− 3.00	192.25	165.85	151

Est vol 6,647; vol Fri 6,396; open int 4,724, −143.
The index: High 175.95; Low 173.07; Close 173.07 −2.88

MAJOR MKT INDEX (CBT) $250 times index

Jan	534.00	535.90	527.60	528.30	−10.30	556.50	508.00	9,096
Feb	532.75	534.75	527.50	527.70	−10.30	554.50	527.50	328
Mar	536.05	536.50	528.75	529.25	−10.35	555.25	529.25	37

Est vol 5,500; vol Fri 4,220; open int 9,461, −33.
The index: High 535.51; Low 526.80; Close 526.86 −8.59

−OTHER INDEX FUTURES−

Settlement price of selected contract. Volume and open interest of all contract months.

KC Mini Value Line (KC)−100 times Index
Mar 236.00 −5.00; Est. vol. 75; Open int. 188
KC Value Line Index (KC)−500 times Index
Mar 236.30 −4.75; Est. vol. 175; Open int. 1,430
The index: High 239.21; Low 235.33; Close 235.33 −3.86
CRB Index (NYFE)−250 times Index
Mar 222.10 +4.70; Est. vol. 875; Open int. 1,027
The index: High 221.67; Low 218.11; Close 221.67 +3.56
NIKKEI 225 Stock Average (CME)−$5 times NSA
Mar 23800.0 −900.0; Est. vol. 575; Open int. 4,156
The index: High 24036.99; Low 23735.59; Close 23736.57 −332.61

CBT−Chicago Board of Trade. CME−Chicago Mercantile Exchange. KC−Kansas City Board of Trade. NYFE−New York Futures Exchange, a unit of the New York Stock Exchange.

FUTURES OPTIONS

S&P 500 STOCK INDEX (CME) $500 times premium

Strike Price	Calls–Settle			Puts–Settle		
	Jan-c	Feb-c	Mr-c	Jan-p	Feb-p	Mar-p
310	10.25	14.80	17.90	2.70	7.30	10.45
315	6.65	11.50	14.70	4.10	8.95	12.20
320	3.90	8.55	11.75	6.35	10.95	14.15
325	1.90	5.95	9.10	9.35	13.35	16.45
330	0.90	3.85	6.80	13.35	16.15	6.80
335	0.35	2.25	4.80	17.75	....	4.80

Est. vol. 6,705; Fri vol. 2,118 calls; 4,095 puts
Open interest Fri; 26,730 calls; 40,726 puts

−OTHER INDEX FUTURES OPTIONS−

NYSE COMPOSITE INDEX (NYFE) $500 times premium

Strike Price	Calls–Settle			Puts–Settle		
	Jan-c	Feb-c	Mar-c	Jan-p	Feb-p	Mar-p
174	2.45	4.80	6.55	3.10	5.35	7.15

Est. vol. 174, Fri vol. 42 calls, 25 puts
Open interest Fri 559 calls, 469 puts

Source: *The Wall Street Journal,* Tuesday, January 8, 1991

Figure 5-21   Redraw the Neckline

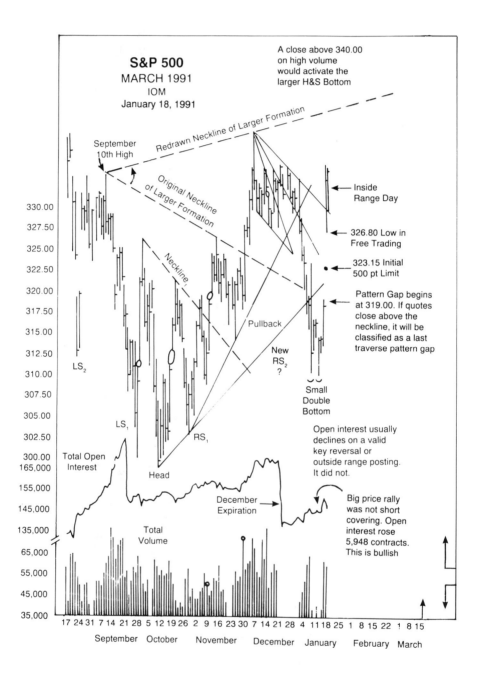

S&P 500
MARCH 1991
IOM
January 18, 1991

A close above 340.00 on high volume would activate the larger H&S Bottom

September 10th High

Redrawn Neckline of Larger Formation

Original Neckline of Larger Formation

Neckline₁

Pullback

New RS₂ ?

Inside Range Day

326.80 Low in Free Trading

323.15 Initial 500 pt Limit

Pattern Gap begins at 319.00. If quotes close above the neckline, it will be classified as a last traverse pattern gap

LS₂

LS₁

Head

RS₁

Small Double Bottom

Open interest usually declines on a valid key reversal or outside range posting. It did not.

Total Open Interest

December Expiration

Big price rally was not short covering. Open interest rose 5,948 contracts. This is bullish

Total Volume

330.00
327.50
325.00
322.50
320.00
317.50
315.00
312.50
310.00
307.50
305.00
302.50
300.00
165,000
155,000
145,000
135,000
65,000
55,000
45,000
35,000

17 24 31 7 14 21 28 5 12 19 26 2 9 16 23 30 7 14 21 28 4 11 18 25 1 8 15 22 1 8 15
September   October   November   December   January   February   March

Pullback Finished: Establish Vertical Bull Call Spread

Thursday, January 24, 1991

An upside breakout from an apparent Bull Flag has occurred. The word "apparent" is used because Flag patterns are not usually found within consolidation areas on a chart. But it certainly appears that the sell-off attempt to fill in the large Pattern Gap at 319.00 on the March S&Ps (Figure 5-23) is over.

Figure 5-22   Redraw the Neckline

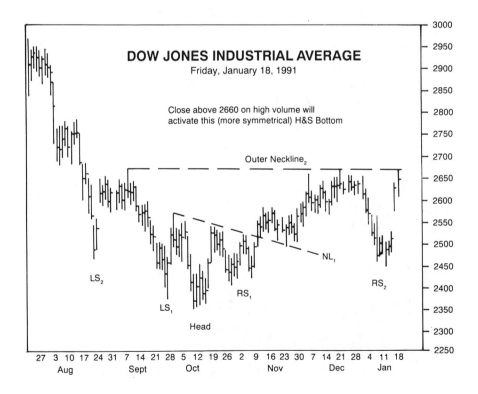

Figure 5-23   Attempt at Pullback to Close Gap Is Finished

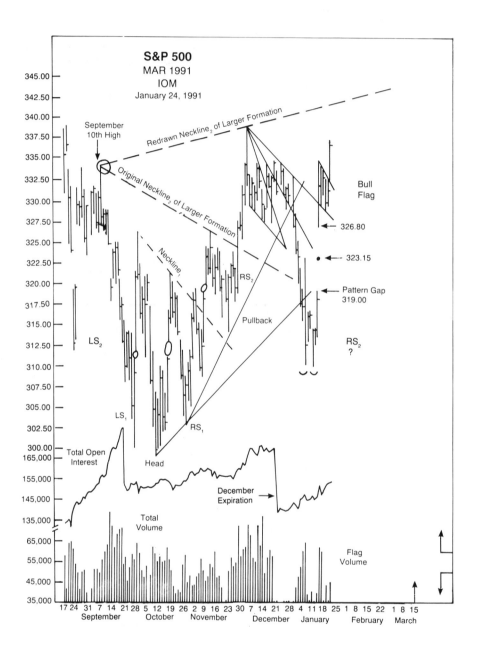

An upside breakout above the neckline of the possible H&S Bottom has not yet occurred. But vertical bull call spreads in the March S&P options are the suggested position.

The long 335 versus short 340 call spread will be monitored. This vertical bull spread is placed using option strikes on either side of the futures 336.80 settlement. This is for liquidity considerations and anticipated follow-up action. The trader will now be holding one long March 335 call and a two-lot long March 335 call versus short March 340 vertical bull call spread.

Option Prices for January 24, 1991

FUTURES OPTIONS

S&P 500 STOCK INDEX (CME) $500 times premium

Strike	Calls—Settle			Puts—Settle		
Price	Feb-c	Mar-c	Ju-c	Feb-p	Mar-p	Jun-p
325	14.60	17.70	26.45	2.85	6.05	12.25
330	10.70	14.10	23.15	3.95	7.35	13.80
335	7.35	10.90	19.95	5.55	9.10	15.45
340	4.60	8.10	16.85	7.80	11.25	17.25
345	2.60	5.80	14.00	10.75	13.90	....
350	1.30	3.75	11.40	14.45	16.85	21.55

Est. vol. 7,354; Wed vol. 1,028 calls; 2,787 puts
Open interest Wed; 27,881 calls; 46,702 puts

Vertical Bull Call Spread

	Price	Implied Volatility	Delta
Long 335 Mar call	10.90	20.3%	+.54
Short 340 Mar call	8.10	19.6%	−.46

Per One-Lot Spread

Cost of spread (in points)	2.80 (debit)
Cost of spread (in U.S. Dollars)	1,400$
Maximum risk (in points)	2.80
Maximum reward (in points)	2.20
Breakeven at expiration (Lower strike + net debit)	337.80
Delta of spread	+0.08

Option Derivatives

Ideally, an options trader will have access to an algorithm to calculate the important derivatives that can be obtained from a theoretical options pricing model. The data in Table 5-10 were produced by the Chicago Mercantile Exchange's Options & Alternatives software. These derivatives are of vital importance in determining the risk of an options position. This is especially true as the strategies become more complicated and involve numerous options. The definitions are listed below.

Delta:

Rate of change of the theoretical option price in relation to the change in the price of the underlying instrument. Delta is expressed in percentage terms.

Gamma:

Rate of change of delta. For an option with a delta of .54 and a gamma of .02, if the price of the underlying goes up one point, the new delta would be .56.

Theta:

The amount of loss of an option's value as a day passes assuming no movement in the underlying price.

Vega:

How an option price reacts to a change in volatility. If implied volatility in an option with a vega of .50 increased by 1 percent, the option would theoretically gain .50 points in price.

Upside Breakout: Remove One-Half of Losing Leg

Wednesday, January 30, 1991

As seen in Figures 5-24 through 5-26, the neckline of the largest H&S Bottom has been redrawn on the March S&P 500, S&P 100 and Dow Industrials charts. Total New York Stock Exchange (NYSE) volume was 226,790,000 shares on Wednesday, January 30, when the Dow Industrials closed above 2660. This was high, but not the 250+ million that technicians would have expected. S&P 500 futures volume moved up to 50,443 but again did not surpass the 60,000-contract breakout hurdle previously set. In addition, the breakout on the March S&P futures was net short covering—open interest

Table 5-10   March 1991 S&P 500 Options

Futures Price 336.8	Estimated Volatility 20.0%	Interest Rate 5.9%	Start Date 01-24-1991	Expiration Date 03-14-1991

Derivatives

Strike Price	Theoretical Premium	Delta	Gamma	Theta	Vega
365.0	1.8	14.3%	0.9%	0.06	0.28
360.0	2.5	19.0%	1.1%	0.07	0.33
355.0	3.5	24.6%	1.3%	0.08	0.39
350.0	4.7	31.0%	1.4%	0.09	0.43
345.0	6.3	38.2%	1.5%	0.10	0.47
340.0	8.3	46.0%	1.6%	0.10	0.49
335.0	10.7	53.9%	1.6%	0.10	0.49
330.0	13.4	61.9%	1.5%	0.09	0.46
325.0	16.6	69.4%	1.4%	0.09	0.43
320.0	20.1	76.3%	1.2%	0.08	0.37
315.0	23.9	82.2%	1.0%	0.06	0.31
310.0	28.1	87.2%	0.8%	0.05	0.25

was down 122 contracts. This does not mean that the H&S Bottoms will not work; it does mean that a pullback to the breakout levels would not be surprising.

Traders with no prior positions and the desire not to miss the possible price move would be buyers of call options on the close Wednesday, January 30. The situation in the March at-the-money calls was:

Index	Close	Change	At-the-Money Call		
S&P 100 (OEX Cash)	323.06	+5.66	Mar S&P 100	325C =	7 3/8
S&P 500 (SPX Cash)	340.91	+5.07	Mar S&P 500	340C =	9 3/4
S&P 500 March Future	342.25	+5.50	Mar S&P 500	340C =	10.15
MMI (XMI Cash)	567.21	+9.40	Mar MMI	565C =	14 1/2

The upside measuring objectives on the various stock index charts are: 3000 on the Dow Industrials, 380 on the March S&P 500 future, 351 on the

Figure 5-24   Upside Breakout from Complex H&S Bottom
Remove One-Half of Losing Leg

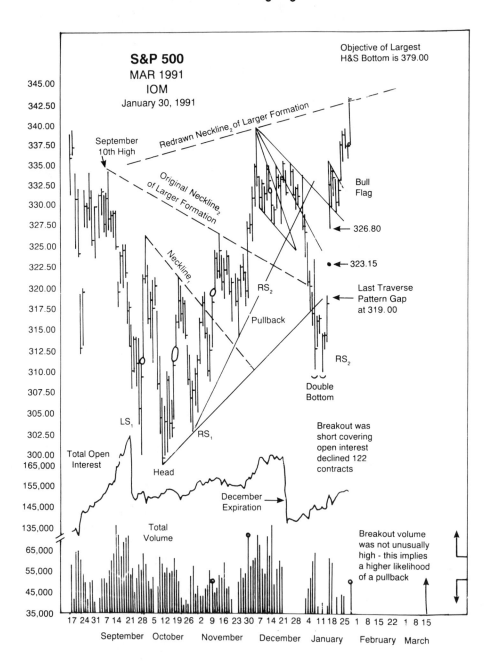

Figure 5-25   Upside Breakout from Complex H&S Bottom

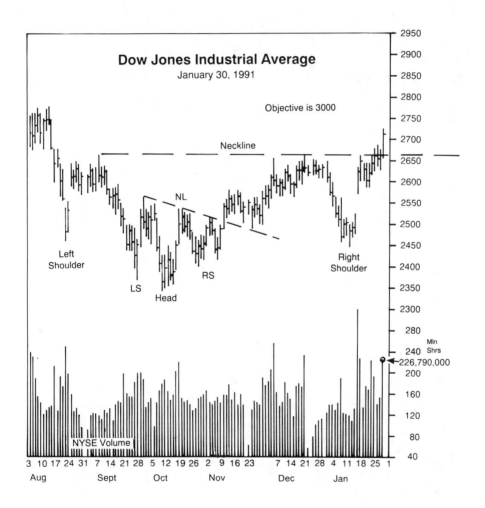

Figure 5-26 Upside Breakout from Complex H&S Bottom

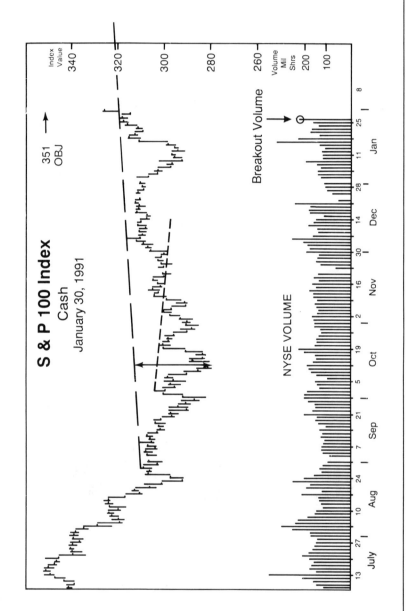

S&P 100 Cash Index, and new highs above 605 in the cash Major Market Index.

Figure 5-27 shows in five-minute intervals how traders reacted to the important (neckline) 2660 level on the Dow Jones Industrial Average. After four trading sessions of flirting with 2660, the official upside breakout took place with the January 30 close.

Traders with vertical bull call spreads would become more aggressive and lift one-half of the losing leg.

Prior Position
Long two Mar 335 calls at 10.90 x 2
Short two Mar 340 calls at 8.10 x 2
Long one Mar 335 call at 12.90

Follow-up: Lift one-half losing leg
Buy one Mar 340 call at 10.15
(for a loss of 8.10 – 10.15 = –2.05)

Present Position
Long two Mar 335 calls
(Open trade profit = (13.40 – 10.90) x 2 = 5.00)
Short one Mar 340 call
(Open trade loss = –2.05)
Long one Mar 335 call
(Open trade profit = 13.40 – 12.90 = 0.50)
Net open trade profit = 3.45

**Figure 5-27   Five-Minute Chart: Dow Jones Industrial Average
Anatomy of a Breakout**

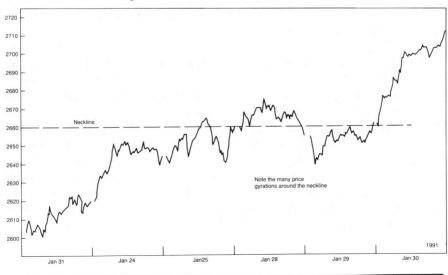

Follow-up

Friday, February 1, 1991

The appearance of the Outside Range Day on the March S&P 500 chart on Friday, February 1 (Figure 5-28), implies that the low of the day will be taken out. If this minor trend change indicator works as expected, a pullback to below the neckline would occur. Note that the price posting can also be described as a Key Reversal Day. This is a new life of contract high followed by a lower close. A Key Reversal is typically a minor trend change indicator; it forecasts a lower price low than the low of the Key Reversal Day.

Classical support is found at 339.00 on the March S&P chart. This is the location of a "former high" on the chart. Support on the DJIA begins at 2675 and extends down to the neckline breakout at 2660. The 2675 support can be seen as the intraday high on January 28 in Figure 5-27. Any price decline on diminishing volume would be an opportunity for buying outright longs and for lifting the remaining one-half losing leg of any vertical bull call spreads.

Elliott Wave Count

Friday, February 15, 1991

An explosive price upmove occurred; no low-volume pullback occurred for a low-risk entry into new longs. Refer to Figure 5-29.

The first minor sign of profit taking by the bulls occurred with the open interest decline of 1,611 contracts (not shown) on Thursday, February 14. But because this signal occurred on a price down day, it is deemed typical of a market experiencing a correction.

One form of technical analysis that deals in depth with corrective price moves is the Elliott Wave Principle. Since corrections are supposed to occur in waves 2 or 4 in an Elliott Wave analysis, the current best count is shown on the chart in Figure 5-29. This wave count implies that at least one more surge to new life of contract highs is needed. This price surge would be labeled impulse wave 5. Technicians would anticipate that this push would carry quotes to at least 379.00 to achieve the H&S Bottom measuring objective.

For futures traders stopped out on the slight dip below support at 365.00, longs should be replaced if Friday's open interest shows a positive change. A positive change would be unusually bullish in the face of the February options series expiration. Futures open interest normally experiences a temporary decline at the expiration of an option series.

Some technicians may be tempted to label the recent week's price activity as a Bull Flag. The problem with this technical interpretation is that the most recent breakout took place on the price move above 365.00. This prior breakout is where the flagpole should start. This does not make sense. There is not enough of a staff from which the Flag can "fly." But much like the price activity back in mid-January, an explosive price up move should occur when quotes trade above 372.00 (a new high). Note that the Elliott Wave count at just below the 335.00 level is also being labeled as a small "iv" wave.

The only technical condition that would turn the chart short-term bearish would be a close below 365.00. Therefore, protective sell-stops for futures traders should be placed at 363.40. Bullish positioned futures and options traders should consider taking at least partial profits at 379.00.

Possible Triangle Forming

Friday, February 22, 1991

The upside measuring objective of 379.00 from the Complex Head & Shoulders Bottom has not yet been achieved.

Three reversals of the minor price trend have formed over the last two weeks. It is technically illegal to use the daily low of Friday, February 22 (Figure 5-30) to construct a trendline. This is because a higher daily low has to be posted before a clear-cut reversal point can be established. Yet an up-sloping minor trendline is (prematurely) shown in Figure 5-30 with the technical expectation that a Symmetrical Triangle could be forming.

A triangular interpretation would fit into a fourth wave (correction) under the Elliott Wave Principle. The fact that Friday's high was out of the upside of the Triangle does not destroy the formation. A *close* beyond a boundary line is needed to activate a Triangle and create a measuring objective.

The height of the Triangle is measured at reversal point 2. This was the daily range on Thursday, February 14 of 8.50 points. The approximate location of the upside breakout is 371.50. Activating a Triangle would create an upside objective on the March S&Ps of 380.00. Refer to Chapter Eight for a more complete explanation of this pattern.

A signal that the correction might be ending was the slight increase in total open interest of 446 contracts on Wednesday, February 21. The open interest increase was associated with a price down day (–3.65). In a most minute analysis, this would be regarded as a sign of a healthy bear market. But notice that open interest had been decreasing during the previous three postings. This is typical of profit taking during a correction. Since the bulls have been the "smart money," the technician should look for a signal that

Figure 5-28   Outside Range Day Implies that a Pullback to Support is Likely

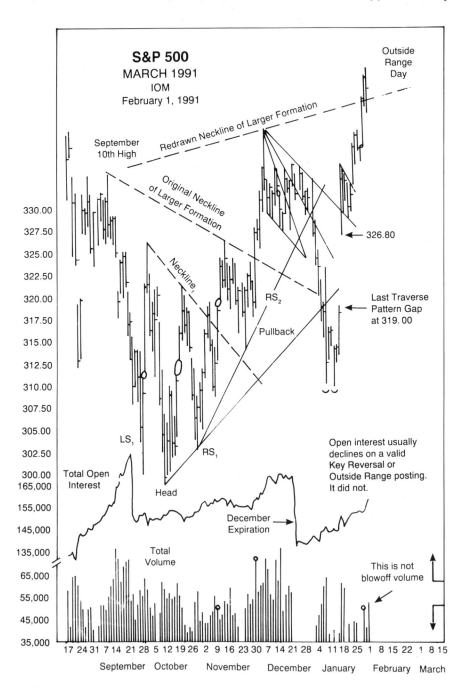

Figure 5-29   Elliott Wave Count During Breakout

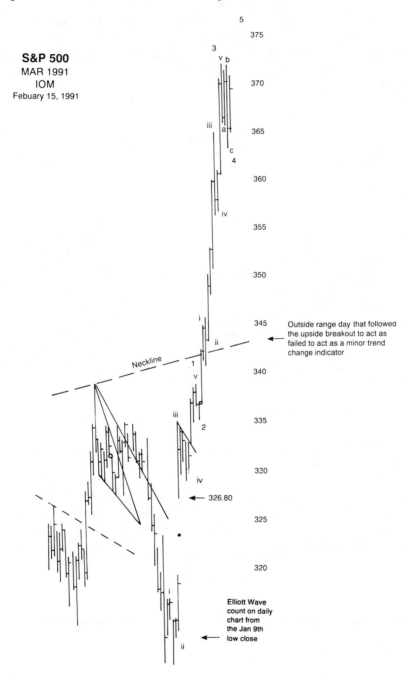

S&P 500
MAR 1991
IOM
Febuary 15, 1991

Neckline

Outside range day that followed
the upside breakout to act as
failed to act as a minor trend
change indicator

← 326.80

Elliott Wave
count on daily
chart from
the Jan 9th
low close

they are returning. The expectation is that open interest will increase along with any new upward push in prices.

An options trader with no open positions might consider a long straddle or more directional call ratio backspread. These strategies are detailed in other case studies in this book. In this case study, traders are already bullishly positioned with a long call and two-lot vertical bull call spread and should maintain that view.

Triangle Failure

Friday, March 1, 1991

The Symmetrical Triangle interpretation posed one week ago did indeed form. But the direction of the breakout was in the low probability direction—to the downside. Options traders with a long-term bullish view have the staying power to monitor this unexpected technical development. Short term, the bearish Triangle could work and then the major bull trend reassert itself. In this case, the bearish Triangle failed. This is shown in the first chart in Figure 5-31 where prices moved back out the upside of the Triangle.

The bearish scenario would be the possible Head & Shoulders Top depicted. Indeed, the price rally of Wednesday, February 27 was short covering—open interest in S&P futures declined 450 contracts (not shown). But the volume was higher than bears would have liked at 63,552 (also not shown).

Now two diametrically opposed chart patterns are shown in Figure 5-31. The bullish position would be the creation of another Symmetrical Triangle. Note that the assumption is being made that Friday's low holds for the fourth reversal point.

From a longer-term technical reading, the outcome on the daily chart should be a Symmetrical Triangle. This is because the minimum measuring objective of the large Head & Shoulders Bottom at 379.00 has yet to be achieved. The Triangle measuring objective is approximately 380.00 if the formation is activated.

Head & Shoulders Bottom Objective Achieved: Take Partial Profits

Wednesday, March 6, 1991

All upside measuring objectives on the Dow Jones Industrial Average chart and the S&P 500 March futures chart were achieved (Figures 5-33 and 5-34).

Figure 5-30   Possible Symmetrical Triangle

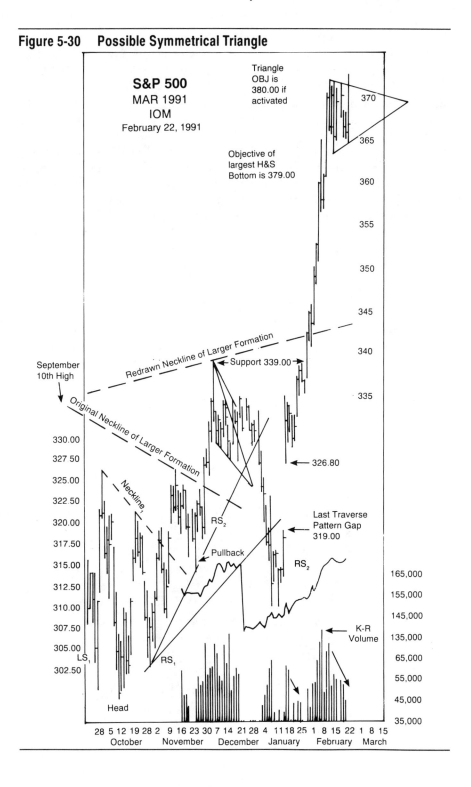

The Dow crossed the psychological 3000 barrier twice intraday (Figure 5-32). A price rally in the last five minutes of trading prevented a Key Reversal high posting on the Dow chart; the close was +0.75 at 2973.27.

The March S&P 500 futures did post a Key Reversal Day, setting a new life of contract high at 380.20 and settling 0.75 lower at 376.60. Ideally, volume on a valid Key Reversal will be of "blowoff" proportion. On a futures chart, total open interest would be expected to decline.

These two internal statistics were available prior to the opening the next trading session. Turnover at 88,932 was indeed extremely high and open interest did decline—down 4,248 contracts. An unchanged opening allowed aggressive short term traders to try to pick a top via short sales.

Longer-term traders with existing bullish positions would take partial profits because the upside measuring objective of the Complex H&S Bottom was finally met. A general rule of thumb is to take profits on one-quarter of the position. Because of the Key Reversal Day, one-half of existing bullish positions should be removed. Options prices for the close March 6 are found in Table 5-11. It is interesting to note that prices for the 335 and 340 strike price calls are not even listed in the newspaper quotations; they are too deep in-the-money!

Table 5-11   Options Prices for Wednesday, March 6, 1991

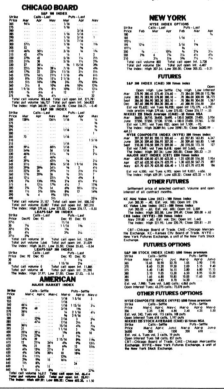

Figure 5-31   Failed Triangle and Two New Possible Formations

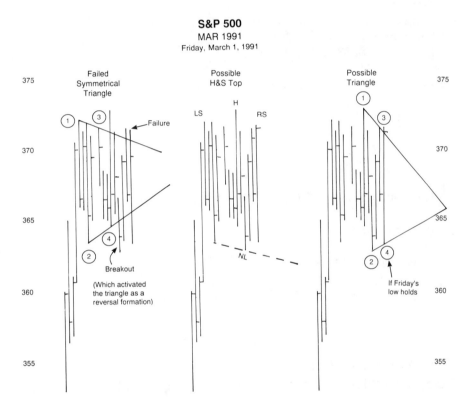

S&P 500
MAR 1991
Friday, March 1, 1991

The March 335 S&P 500 calls settled at 41.60; exactly equal to their intrinsic value (376.60 – 335 = 41.60). This is expected since these options expire in several days and little time value is left. The results use the closing prices for March 6. The 376.60 settlement price on the March future was 2.40 below the 379.00 H&S Bottom objective and 3.40 below the 380.00 Triangle objective which were both met in intraday trading on March 6.

Prior Position
Long two Mar 335 calls at 10.90
Short one Mar 340 call at 8.10
Long one Mar 335 call at 12.90

Follow-up: Leave one long call open, liquidate remainder of position
Sell two Mar 335 calls at 41.60
(for a profit of (41.60 – 10.90) x 2 = 61.40)

Buy one Mar 340 call at 36.70
(for a loss of 8.10 – 36.70 = –28.60)

Net result = (61.40 – 28.60) x 500$ = 16,400$

Present Position
Long one Mar 335 call
Open trade profit = 41.60 – 12.90 = 28.70

Figure 5-32   Dow Jones Industrial Average at Five-Minute Intervals on Wednesday, March 6, 1991

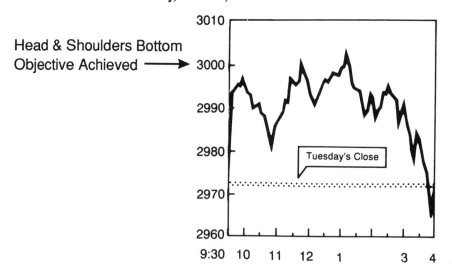

Head & Shoulders Bottom
Objective Achieved ⟶

Figure 5-33   H&S Bottom Measuring Objective Met

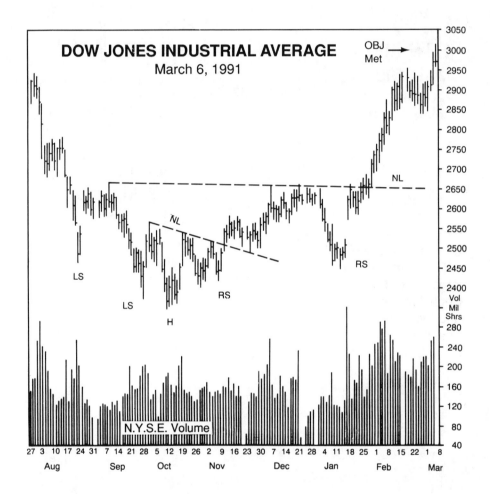

Figure 5-34   H&S Bottom Measuring Objective Met: Take Partial Profits

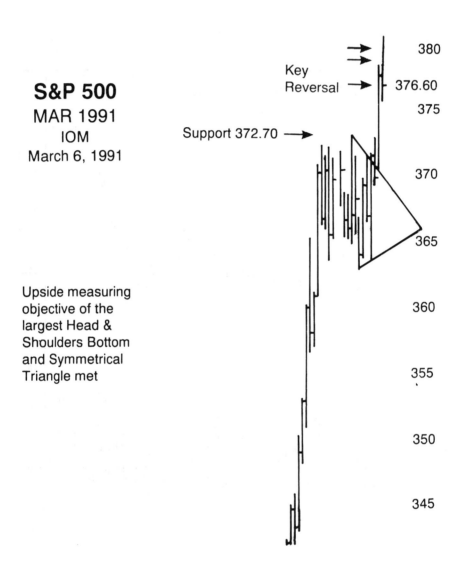

S&P 500
MAR 1991
IOM
March 6, 1991

Key
Reversal → 376.60

Support 372.70 →

380
375
370
365
360
355
350
345

Upside measuring
objective of the
largest Head &
Shoulders Bottom
and Symmetrical
Triangle met

Locating Underlying Support

The task of the technical trader now becomes one of locating the probable position of underlying support. This is necessary to know when to liquidate the remaining long call position.

Figure 5-35   Locating Support

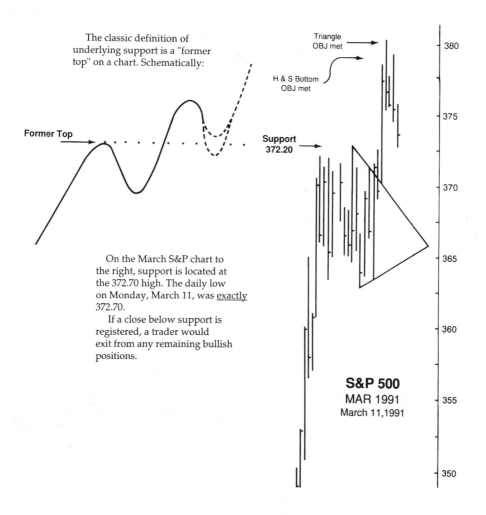

The classic definition of underlying support is a "former top" on a chart. Schematically:

Former Top

Triangle OBJ met

H & S Bottom OBJ met

Support 372.20

On the March S&P chart to the right, support is located at the 372.70 high. The daily low on Monday, March 11, was <u>exactly</u> 372.70.

If a close below support is registered, a trader would exit from any remaining bullish positions.

S&P 500
MAR 1991
March 11,1991

Support Violated: Remove All Remaining Positions

Tuesday, March 12, 1991

Figure 5-36 shows that the support was violated by a close (370.85) below the 372.70 support on the March S&P chart. This dictated removing all remaining long positions.

```
S&P 500 STOCK INDEX (CME) $500 times premium
Strike      Calls-Settle              Puts-Settle
Price    Mar-c  Apr-c   Ju-c  Mar-p   Apr-p   Jun-p
360      11.20  17.20   21.20   0.35   3.10    7.30
365       6.70  13.45   17.75   0.85   4.35    8.80
370       3.00  10.15   14.65   2.15   6.00   10.50
375       1.00   7.40   11.90   5.15   8.20   12.70
380       0.25   5.15    9.55   9.40  10.90   15.20
385       0.05   3.45    7.45  14.15  14.15   18.00
Est. vol. 4,479; Mon vol. 1,186 calls; 2,904 puts
Open Interest Mon; 43,152 calls; 77,653 puts
```

Sell one Mar 335 call at 35.85 (intrinsic value)
(for a profit of 35.85 – 12.90 = 22.95)

OVERALL RESULTS OF CASE STUDIES 1 AND 2

December Options Net Result:	=	+9.40	(page 5-57)
March Options:			
Loss on one long 335 call	=	–8.10	(page 5-64)
Loss on one short 340 call	=	–2.05	(page 5-75)
Profit on two long 335 calls	=	+61.40	(page 5-84)
Loss on one short 340 call	=	–28.60	(page 5-84)
Profit on one long 335 call	=	+22.95	(page 5-88)
		+55.00	

55.00 x 500 $US = 27,500 $US
(profit before commissions)

The two case studies covered a time span of four months and two options expiration series. There was some technical disappointment when the Head

Figure 5-36   Support Violated: Remove All Remaining Positions

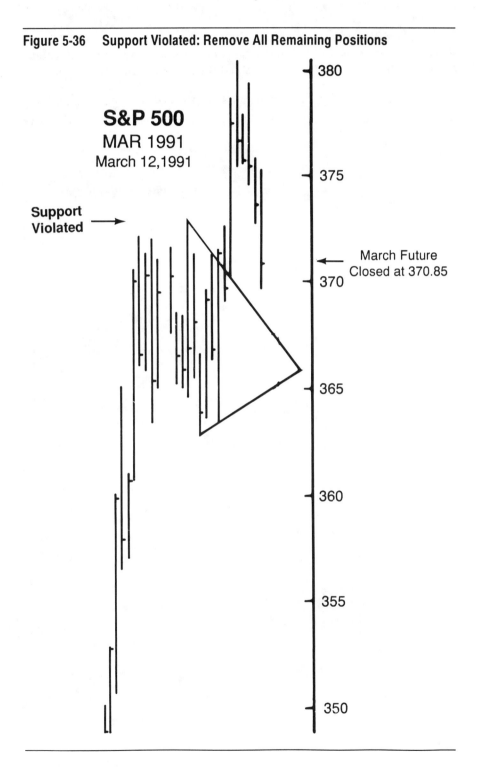

S&P 500
MAR 1991
March 12, 1991

Support Violated →

← March Future
Closed at 370.85

& Shoulders Bottom appeared to be failing. The discipline required to be a successful trader was illustrated when the neckline had to be relocated. Acting on this new development enabled the overall technical campaign to be a very profitable one.

Figure 5-37 shows the S&P 500 chart on the opening Friday, March 15, when both the future and its options expired. The cash settlement price was 374.91.

Figure 5-37   March Expiration

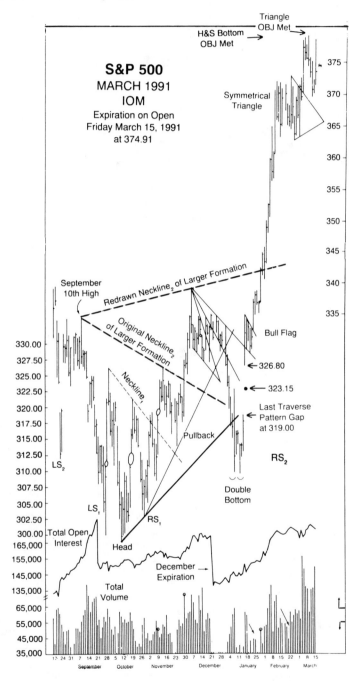

S&P 500
MARCH 1991
IOM
Expiration on Open
Friday March 15, 1991
at 374.91

CHAPTER **6**

POSSIBLE HEAD & SHOULDERS BOTTOM

SYNTHETIC LONG CALL

Options Strategy	When to Use	Technical Situation
Synthetic Long Call	When most bullish	A gap open is likely to exceed a normal futures sell-stop order (report due)

A synthetic option is a position that replicates a specific option using other financial instruments. Creating synthetic positions is the bailiwick of the arbitrage traders. These professional traders, taking advantage of any mispricings, use synthetics to keep the relationships between options and the underlying market in line.

Is a synthetic position of any use to a position trader with a definite directional bias? The case study in this chapter will investigate the use of a synthetic long call in a near-to-expire option series. The outcome of a traditional vertical bull call spread (using the next expiration series) will also be investigated. Both of these option strategies will then be compared to an outright long position in the underlying instrument.

June and September '87 T-Bond Case Study

A bar chartist looking at the June 1987 Chicago Board of Trade (CBOT) U.S. Treasury Bond chart in Figure 6-1 would want to be long T-bonds. It certainly

appears that a Head & Shoulders Bottom is forming on the chart. A long
futures position could be protected with a sell-stop-loss order. This is the
typical means of limiting a loss. But when the protection of a stop order is
needed most, prices are often moving violently. The resulting fill is the best
prevailing price at the time, but quite often substantially through the stop
price.

This case study will investigate the use of a long put option for an
"optional stop" to protect a long position in the underlying instrument. The
important technical considerations and statistics are listed below.

Given

1. Going into close of trading Tuesday, May 5, 1987.

2. Entering an important quarterly U.S. Treasury refunding
    (nervous market).

3. There have been two recent increases in the U.S. prime rate.

4. Symmetrical Triangle downside objective on Eurodollar
    Time Deposit futures chart not yet achieved (not shown).
    Note: This implies the Eurodollar chart is bearish.

5. Outside Range Day on September T-bond chart (Figure 6-2)
    is a minor trend change indicator and a right shoulder low
    of an H&S Bottom may be in place.

6. Symmetry with the possible left shoulder suggests an upside
    breakout by Friday, May 15.

Statistics

1. Date: Tuesday, May 5, 1987

2. June option last trading day: May 15 (10 days)

3. September option last trading day: August 21 (107 days)

4. Futures close:

    June: 91-19
    September: 90-19

5. Options prices for close May 5, 1987 were:

T-BONDS (CBT) $100,000; points and 64ths of 100%

Strike Price	Calls—Last			Puts—Last		
	Jun-c	Sep-c	Dec-c	Jun-p	Sep-p	Dec-p
88	3-52	4-45	4-61	0-14	2-12	3-16
90	2-15	3-31	3-47	0-38	2-59	4-00
92	1-01	2-31	2-42	1-25	3-50	5-00
94	0-25	1-44	2-00	2-50	4-60	6-07
96	0-09	1-05	1-26	4-34	6-17	7-33
98	0-03	0-37	0-53	6-28	7-53	8-58

Est. vol. 93,000, Mon vol. 37,739 calls, 51,819 puts
Open interest Mon; 376,609 calls, 259,562 puts

Note: Quotes are in 64ths - 1/64 = 15.625 $US

Figure 6-1   Possible Head & Shoulders Bottom

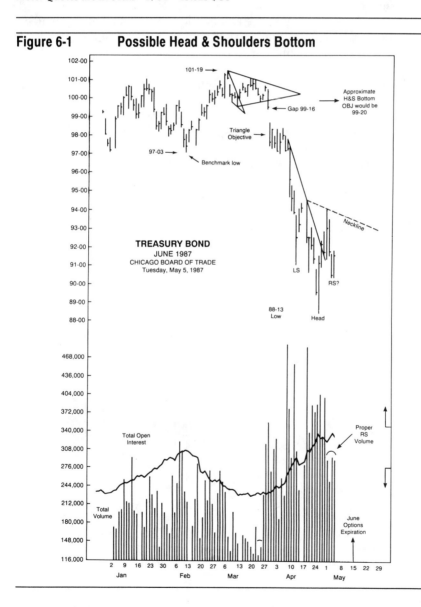

TRADING PLAN

The June T-bond call options expire in only ten days. This is too soon to expect the developing H&S Bottom to form and meet its upside measuring objective. But by the time ten days pass, the probable outcome on the chart—specifically whether an upside breakout has occurred—should be known.

An aggressive trader who really wants to be long futures should need tight stop-loss protection only until the bullish pattern is officially activated. Buying put options to mitigate the risk in a long futures position creates a synthetic long call. This position's risk/reward diagram is similar in shape to that of a long call. This will be discussed in detail in conjunction with the diagram in Figure 6-5.

If the upside breakout does occur, quotes will have moved up from the 91-19 level at which the long futures position was placed on May 5. The long put options will expire and then a traditional sell-stop order can be entered in the futures market to protect the long (profitable) futures position.

Figure 6-2   Possible Head & Shoulders Bottom

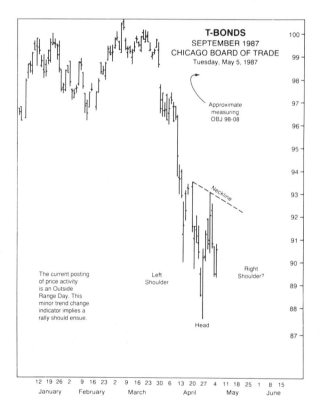

The September T-bond chart in Figure 6-2 also contains the possibility that an H&S Bottom is forming. Since the September options expire in 107 days, options traders using traditional vertical bull call spreads have ample time to use their favorite strategy of leading off. Three vertical spreads are detailed in Figure 6-4. Their outcome will be compared to the outcome of the synthetic long call strategy as well as to simply going long the June futures.

OPTIONS EXPIRATIONS

Some futures contracts require physical delivery if positions are held to expiration. Knowledge of *when* an option expires is obviously crucial. Options on futures contracts that require physical delivery must expire before first notice day. This means that the Chicago Board of Trade's futures options (T-bonds, corn, wheat, etc.) expire in the month *prior to* the expiration month of the future.

In the case of foreign exchange futures on the International Monetary Market division of the Chicago Mercantile Exchange, physical delivery does take place. But the delivery day is two business days *following* the expiration of the future. The options on the D-Mark, for example, do expire in the same month as the futures, but earlier than the futures expire. It is imperative to know the contract specifications before trading anything. Time lines illustrating the important features of the T-bond and D-Mark futures and options are diagrammed below.

U.S. Treasury Bond Futures (CBOT)

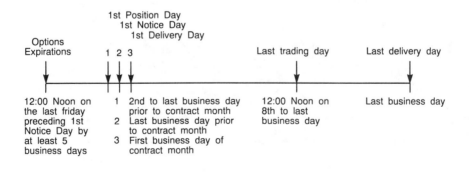

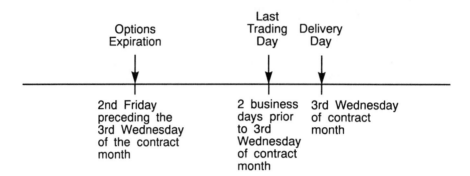

Deutsche Mark Futures (IMM)

IMPLIED VOLATILITY CONSIDERATIONS

The implied volatility chart of T-bond call options is shown in Figure 6-3. Volatility on May 5 looks relatively high (17+ percent). Traditional option pricing models infer that spreaders should have a bias toward selling the at-the-money calls. These are the Sept 90 calls. This would be the short leg of any spread. Therefore, the long leg of a vertical bull call spread (established for volatility reasons) would be the purchase of the in-the-money Sept

Figure 6-3   Implied Volatility Chart: T-Bond Calls

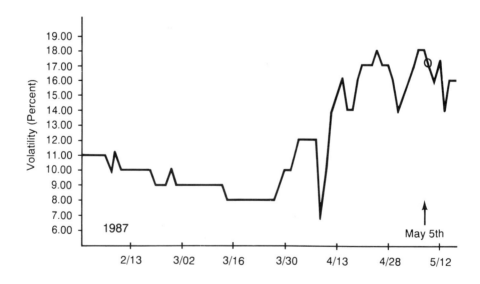

**Figure 6-4   Risk/Reward Diagrams of Vertical Bull Call Spreads
September 1990 T-Bond Futures Options
at Expiration**

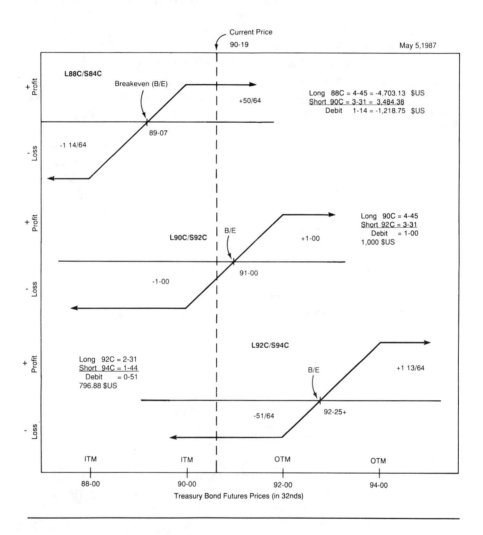

88 calls. The risk/reward diagram of the L88/S90 call spread as well as two additional bull spreads are plotted in Figure 6-4.

Traders contemplating the purchase of put options to protect outright longs in the underlying instrument would want to examine an implied volatility chart of the puts. Ideally implied volatility would be average or below so the purchase of puts for protection would not be too expensive. Volatility forecasting is examined in more detail in Chapter Fifteen.

OPTIONS PRICES

The minimum price fluctuation of a CBOT T-bond option is 1/64. This represents a U.S. Dollar value of 15.625$ (rounded to 15.63$) on one option contract. The Dollar values of 1/64 to 64/64 are listed in Table 6-1. The minimum price fluctuation on the underlying instrument, the T-bond future, is 1/32 or 31.25$ on one contract.

Since the delta of an at-the-money option is very close to 0.5, a 1/32 point move in the T-bond would theoretically translate into a 1/64 point move in the at-the-money put or call. This configuration of minimum permissible price moves allows the options price to be finely tuned. All the CBOT options are traded in this fashion.

The minimum price fluctuation on Eurodollar options (IMM) or gold options (Comex) is of the same magnitude as the underlying instrument. Why? Each exchange creates its own products and contract specifications. Again, it pays to study before placing orders.

SYNTHETIC LONG CALL

A long June T-bond future at 91-19 is the desired position. The selection of which put option to purchase for protection is analogous to insurance policies with various deductibles. In this case study, the in-the-money June 92-00 strike put will be purchased. The cost of the "insurance" is 1 25/64 or 1,390.63$ and provides immediate protection.

Long one June future at 91-19
Long one June 92-00 put at 1 25/64

The risk/reward diagram of this synthetic long call is seen in Figure 6-5. The shape is similar to that of a long call.

The synthetic long call produces an "optional stop" order at 92-00. A move below the stop does not take the trader out of the position, but risk is mitigated. The maximum loss is equal to the difference between the futures price (91-19) and the put strike (92-00) plus the premium paid: (91-19 - 92-00) + 1 25/64 = 63/64.

Figure 6-5 shows the breakeven point for the position. This is the price of the long future (91-19) plus the put premium (1 25/64) = 92-31+.* Therefore, this strategy does not produce profits at expiration unless the June bonds are above 92-31+. The protection is only good for ten days until Friday, May 15. But by this time the pattern will have evolved enough to ascertain if a long futures position is justified.

---

* T-bond traders operating in 32nds but needing to show an additional 64th added to a particular price indicate this with a +.

Table 6-1   Dollar Value of T-Bond Option Premiums

1/64	$15.63	33/64	515.63
2/64	31.25	34/64	531.25
3/64	46.88	35/64	546.88
4/64	62.50	36/64	562.50
5/64	78.13	37/64	578.13
6/64	93.75	38/64	593.75
7/64	109.38	39/64	609.38
8/64	125.00	40/64	625.00
9/64	140.63	41/64	640.63
10/64	156.25	42/64	656.25
11/64	171.88	43/64	671.88
12/64	187.50	44/64	687.50
13/64	203.13	45/64	703.13
14/64	218.75	46/64	718.75
15/64	234.38	47/64	734.38
16/64	250.00	48/64	750.00
17/64	265.63	49/64	765.63
18/64	281.25	50/64	781.25
19/64	296.88	51/64	796.88
20/64	312.50	52/64	812.50
21/64	328.13	53/64	828.13
22/64	343.75	54/64	843.75
23/64	359.38	55/64	859.38
24/64	375.00	56/64	875.00
25/64	390.63	57/64	890.63
26/64	406.25	58/64	906.25
27/64	421.88	59/64	921.88
28/64	437.50	60/64	937.50
29/64	453.13	61/64	953.13
30/64	468.75	62/64	968.75
31/64	484.38	63/64	984.38
32/64	500.00	64/64	1,000.00

Option premiums will be quoted in 64ths. To determine the dollar value of an option premium, multiply the number of 64ths by $15.625 and round up to the nearest $.01. First determine the price per contract, then multiply by the number of contracts to determine the dollar value of an option position. For example, a premium of 2-37/64 equals $2578.13 per contract. The table may be used as a reference.

Figure 6-5   Risk/Reward Diagram of Synthetic Long Call at Expiration

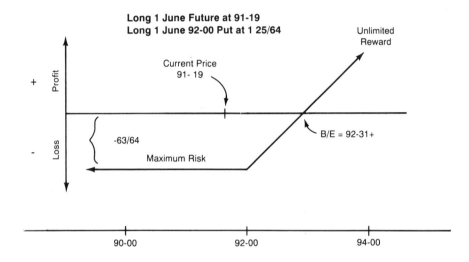

OUTCOME

Figure 6-6 shows that the possible Head & Shoulders Bottom technical interpretation suffered a devastating blow on the day the June T-bond options expired, May 15. A sharply lower price when trading resumed created a Suspension Gap. This would have been through (below) any reasonably placed sell-stop-loss orders in the June T-bond futures.

This was not a Head & Shoulders Bottom pattern failure. The potentially bullish formation was never activated by a close above the neckline. Any bullish strategy attempting to lead off on the potential pattern would have suffered a loss.

Figure 6-6   June Option Expiration

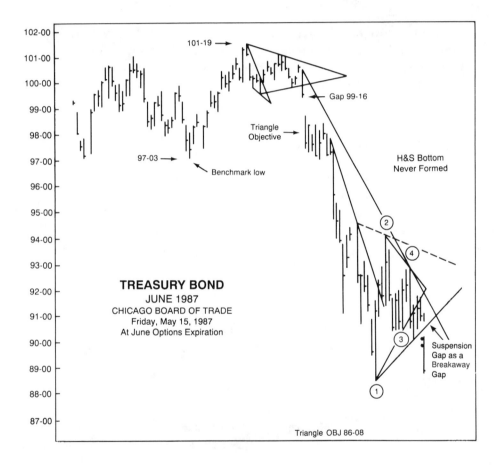

Results of Various Strategies
May 15, 1987 (June Option Expiration)

Long Futures

Long June T-bond	=	91-19
Stopped out	=	90-02
Result	=	-1-17 = -1,531.25$

The June T-bond futures had an unusually wide (90-07 to 89-30) resumption range on the morning of May 15. This was due to resting sell-stop orders being activated. The sell-stops were located just below a two-point trendline on the chart. A price of 90-02 would be representative of a fill received on such a stop.

Synthetic Long Call

Long June T-bond from 91-19	=	-2 23/32
Long June 92-00 put	=	+3 8/64
Initial debit	=	-1 25/64
Result	=	-63/64 = -984.38$

This result uses the settlement price of 88-28 for the June futures on May 15. How is the synthetic long call position unwound? The trader will exercise the long put. This results in a short June futures position at 92-00. The CBOT Clearing Corporation computer will offset this position with the existing long June futures and the account will be even—no open positions.

Vertical Bull Call Spread

Spread	Difference May 5	Difference May 15		Result
L88/S90	On at 1-14	Off at 0-58	=	-20/64 = -312.50$
L90/S92	On at 1-00	Off at 0-47	=	-17/64 = -256.63$
L92/S94	On at 0-51	Off at 0-32	=	-19/64 = -296.88$

Although losses were recorded in all the spreads, remember that the technician was leading off—attempting to pick the bottom of a right shoulder. The limited risk aspect of the vertical spread is the desired attribute when leading off. Because this was a debit spread, the amount of the maximum possible loss was already debited from the account. Since the spreads had not declined to a differential of zero (representing the maximum loss), some funds were returned to the trading account.

SUMMARY

This case study tabulated the results of three distinct strategies for leading off in anticipation that a Head & Shoulders Bottom pattern was forming. It is not surprising that an outright long position in the underlying instrument produced the worst results.

The synthetic long call also produced a loss, but using the put option as a protective stop-loss order was not as damaging.

The most conservative approach to this particular technical situation was the pure option strategy. The vertical bull call spreads still lost money, but the loss, even on the recommended minimum two-lot spread, was the smallest. And follow-up action to make the vertical spread more aggressive was always present—if conditions had warranted.

Figure 6-7 shows the next two weeks of price activity in the June T-bond futures following the May 15 quarterly options expiration. It proved to be a difficult time for all traders.

Figure 6-7   How It Came Out

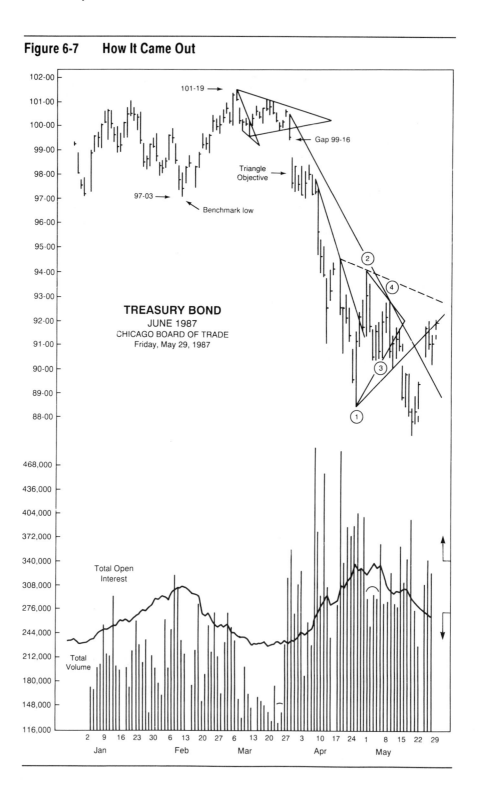

TREASURY BOND
JUNE 1987
CHICAGO BOARD OF TRADE
Friday, May 29, 1987

CHAPTER 7

POSSIBLE HEAD & SHOULDERS TOP

VERTICAL BEAR PUT SPREAD

Options Strategy	When to Use	Technical Situation
Vertical Bear Put Spread	Market expected to fall somewhat	Lead off in anticipation of downside breakout (prior to breaking neckline of a possible H&S Top)

The vertical bear spread using put options will be examined in this chapter. This is a debit spread that will be used to lead off with a directional view in anticipation that a Head & Shoulders Top will form.

U.S. Treasury bond futures will be the underlying instrument. The case study will also examine evening trading on the Chicago Board of Trade. The use of an hourly bar chart will be illustrated as an aid in predicting that a larger pattern (an H&S Top) would be activated on the daily bar chart.

March '88 T-Bond Case Study

Following is an overview of the technical and fundamental considerations affecting the T-bond chart in Figure 7-1:

Given

1. Date: Monday, December 7, 1987.

2. There has been an explosive price upmove in U.S. Treasury bonds in a"flight to quality." This coincided with and followed the world equity market crash of 1987.

3. In reaction to problems of equity market making firms, the U. S. Federal Reserve flooded the U.S. economy with liquidity.

4. U.S. Treasury bonds (and short-term instruments) moved up sharply in price. This took place with massive short covering in T-bond futures; total open interest declined.

5. Total open interest in T-bond futures on the Chicago Board of Trade stopped declining on December 2, 1987. The resulting level of open interest, in effect, returned to the "steady state" level seen prior to the previous price decline (not shown).

6. The price bottom was on Monday, October 19, 1987. This was the day of the colossal 508 point (22.6 percent) plunge in the Dow Jones Industrial Average.

7. After five weeks of choppy T-bond price activity, a rally for a right shoulder of a possible Head & Shoulders Top occurred. On an hourly bar chart (Figure 7-2), this rally took the form of a Rising Wedge (bearish) pattern.

8. Trend followers are long T-bond futures. Their moving average models dictate that sell-stop-close-only orders be placed at 85-24 in the March contract. This price level is so close to the neckline of the impending Head & Shoulders Top that these purely mathematical forces will be responsible for much of the selling pressure if the neckline is broken.

9. The currently all-important merchandise trade statistics (given the present weakness in the U.S. Dollar) will be released on Thursday, December 10 (three trading sessions from now).

10. U.S. economic statistics were released one-half hour prior to the opening of the CBOT T-bond futures in 1987. This often caused gap openings. Subsequent to this case study, the finacial futures in the U.S. began trading ten minutes *before* the release of important economic news.

Figure 7-1   Possible Head & Shoulders Top

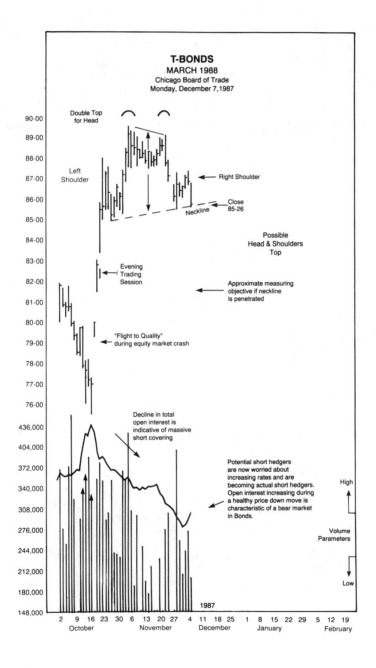

TRADING PLAN

The neckline of the possible H&S Top formation has not been penetrated. The classical bar chart technician (without the benefit of the hourly chart in Figure 7-2) must wait until a close below the neckline is recorded before placing outright short futures positions.

The Rising Wedge formation on the hourly bar chart is a bearish formation. The minimum downside measuring objective is to trade (not necessarily close) below reversal point one. This strongly suggests to a technical trader that the larger formation on the daily chart, the potential H&S Top, will be activated.

Figure 7-2   Hourly Bar Chart - March T-Bonds

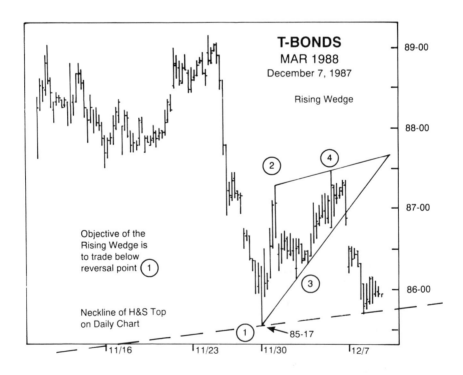

An aggressive options trader would initiate a vertical bear put spread at this time—buy a higher strike, sell a lower strike for a debit spread. In this particular case study, a very conservative approach will be taken. A vertical bear put spread will be initiated only if the neckline is broken by a close below it.

During trading the next session Tuesday, December 8, March T-bond futures moved below 85-17. This satisfied the measuring objective of the Rising Wedge on the hourly chart. Since the location of the close at 85-15 was below the neckline of the Head & Shoulders Top on the daily chart, the bear spread will be placed. Risk/reward diagrams for two possible spreads are shown in Figure 7-3.

Statistics

1. March T-bond futures close = 85-15.

2. Options prices for close Tuesday, December 8, 1987 were:

T-BONDS (CBT) $100,000; points and 64ths of 100%

Strike	Calls–Last			Puts–Last		
Price	Mar-c	Jun-c	Sep-c	Mar-p	Jun-p	Sep-p
82	4-36	4-45	....	1-13	2-14	....
84	3-10	3-28	....	1-44	2-56	....
86	1-63	2-30	....	2-34	3-54	....
88	1-08	1-46	2-20	3-40	5-00	....
90	0-45	1-12	....	5-06	....	....
92	0-24	0-55	....	6-50	8-00	....

Est. vol. 35,000, Mon vol. 21,451 calls, 17,094 puts
Open interest Mon; 205,388 calls, 160,204 puts

---

3. From a typical options valuation model (March options):

	Delta	Implied Volatility	Gamma
ITM 88 put	-.61	15.0	.06
ATM 86 put	-.50	14.5	.06
OTM 84 put	-.38	15.2	.06

4. Vertical Bear Put Spreads

	S84/L86	S86/L88
Cost (debit)	54/64	1 6/64
Delta (of spread)	-.12	-.11
Dollar cost per spread	843.75$	1,093.75$
Maximum risk	843.75$	1,093.75$
Maximum reward	1,156.25$	906.25$
Breakeven price at expiration (higher strike minus net debit)	85-05	86-29

Figure 7-3   Risk/Reward Diagrams
Vertical Bear Put Spreads at Expiration

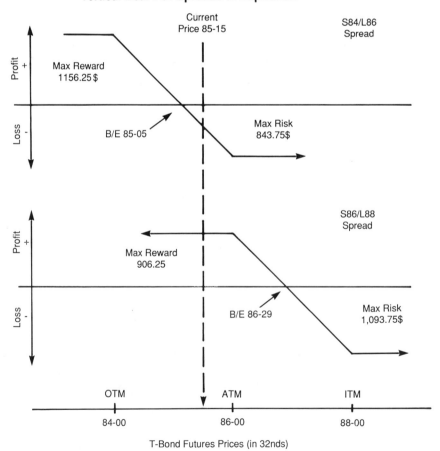

PULLBACK

A price rally on Tuesday, December 15 took March T-bond futures quotes back up toward the neckline at 85-28 (Figure 7-4). The daily high was 85-24 with a settlement price of 85-23 (+50/32). The volume did not appear to be

Figure 7-4   Pullback to the Neckline of an H&S Top

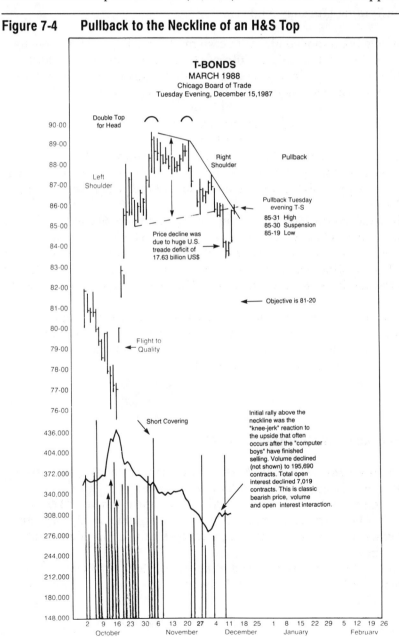

high. Actual volume would not be known with certainty until about noon
local time the next day.

Evening Trading (Tuesday Night)

The long bond moved higher in cash market trading on Tuesday afternoon (after the 2:00 PM Chicago futures close). This caused T-bond futures
in the CBOT Tuesday evening session to trade slightly higher. The range on
March T-bonds in evening trade was:

85-31 high

85-30 suspension (+7/32)

85-19 low

This was the official beginning of Wednesday's trade and can be seen in
Figure 7-4. Note that quotes were higher than the fail-safe trendline drawn
tangent to the price high of the second head and the price high of the right
shoulder.

Is price action during the evening session indicative of continued price
behavior? Should bear positions be abandoned? The first evening session
in the CBOT T-bond futures was April 30, 1987. In the subsequent seven and
one-half months, the evening session proved to be a false indication of future
price direction in more cases than not. This observation continues to be
valid.

If T-bonds were merely pulling back to the neckline, prices should move
lower on Wednesday morning. In addition, a preliminary indication of
Tuesday's actual volume would be available prior to the 8:00 AM (in 1988)
Chicago resumption of trade on Wednesday.

Volume Update (Wednesday Morning)

Cleared volume as of 5:00 PM (the previous afternoon) is available by
telephone by calling the CBOT Midis Touch System.*

Entering the appropriate code yielded a volume estimate of 249,648 for
Tuesday's T-bond trade. Given the 50-tick rally, volume of this magnitude
is no higher than average. This supports the Head & Shoulders pullback
interpretation.

Note: Actual volume, released at approximately 12:00 noon, showed
volume was 247,214. Open interest decreased 6,488 contracts. It was a short
covering rally.

*Refer to Appendix D for 24-hour recorded message telephone numbers.

March 84-00 Put Options

For traders not positioned on the bear side of the T-bonds, the pullback to the neckline was an opportunity to place new positions. It was also a situation where previous bear strategies could be made more bearish.

T-bond futures *resumed* (8:00 AM) trading at 85-29 to 30. The high of the resumption range was 85-30, and quotes moved lower in the first few minutes of trading.

Mar 84 T-bond puts settled at 1-25 on Tuesday. In Tuesday evening's session they traded as low as 1-20. On the steady to slightly lower futures resumption Wednesday morning, the Mar 84 puts traded as low as 1-17. Orders to buy at-the-market would have been filled at 1-20.

OUTCOME OF THE HEAD & SHOULDERS TOP

The Head & Shoulders Top price pattern failed. Quotes took out the high of the head without achieving the minimum measuring objective. Although this pattern is usually very reliable, Figure 7-5 does show one of the cases in which a H&S Top resulted in a failure.

Vertical bear spreads would have been removed to salvage any remaining premium. The prices as of January 5 are listed below.

T-BONDS (CBT) $100,000; points and 64ths of 100%

Strike	Calls—Last			Puts—Last		
Price	Mar-c	Jun-c	Sep-c	Mar-p	Jun-p	Sep-p
84	5-27	5-30	5-20	0-34	1-42	2-22
86	3-55	4-10	4-10	0-57	2-14	....
88	2-23	2-60	3-12	1-29	2-62	....
90	1-25	2-05	....	2-31	4-03	....
92	0-51	1-30	2-00	3-55	5-28	....
94	0-28	1-03	1-28	5-30	....	....

Est. vol. 45,000, Mon vol. 29,429 calls, 21,192 puts
Open interest Mon; 222,519 calls, 186,828 puts

Unwinding the Bear Put Spreads:

	Entry	Exit	Result
S84/L86	0-54	0-23	- 0-31 = - 484.38$
S86/L88	1-06	0-36	- 0-34 = - 531.25$

POSTSCRIPT

Note that the close on the March T-bonds in Figure 7-5 was not above the high of the head. This means there is no technical reason to think that an upside breakout has taken place. Thus, a trader would *not* reverse positions to a bull strategy. Options give staying power, allowing the trader to make the market prove that (in this case) all bearish connotations have been destroyed.

Figure 7-5   Head & Shoulders Top Failure

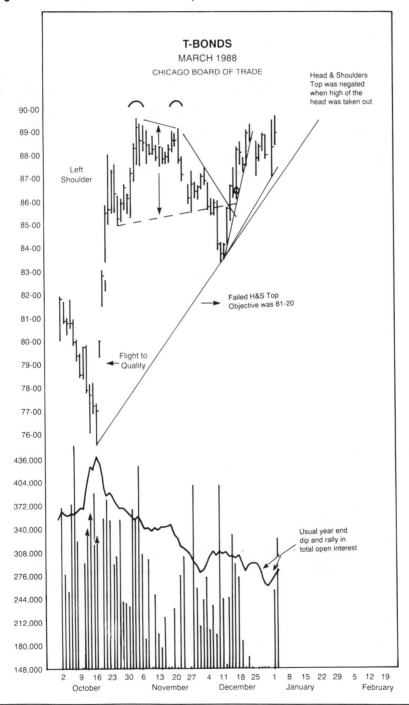

T-BONDS
MARCH 1988
CHICAGO BOARD OF TRADE

Head & Shoulders
Top was negated
when high of the
head was taken out

Left
Shoulder

Failed H&S Top
Objective was 81-20

Flight to
Quality

Usual year end
dip and rally in
total open interest

CHAPTER 8

THEORETICAL EXAMPLE: SYMMETRICAL TRIANGLE

A market is not always making a top or bottom. The most classic technical form that a market takes when moving sideways is a Triangle. The Symmetrical Triangle formation can be either a continuation or reversal pattern. However, historical observation suggests that this price pattern is a continuation pattern with approximately 75 percent probability. This means that prices would be expected to continue in the same direction they were moving when they entered the formation.

Conservative technicians with access only to strategies with unlimited risk (outright long or short) must wait for a Triangle to form—and then enter small (50 percent) positions on the breakout. For a Triangle in a bull market, analysis of volume must show a noticeable increase on the upside breakout. In a futures market, an additional bullish signal would be an increase in open interest. If the proper internal conditions are met, the remainder of speculative long positions can be placed on a pullback to the Triangle breakout, if one occurs.

Figures 8-1 and 8-2 are schematic diagrams of a Symmetrical Triangle in an uptrend and downtrend. The determination of the measuring objective using both a height and parallel line method are shown and, in parentheses, the probability of the breakout direction is indicated. Overall, the Symmetrical Triangle has a reliability of meeting its measuring objective of approximately 75 percent.

The remainder of this chapter is a general outline of the Symmetrical Triangle's technical characteristics and options strategies that will be investigated in Chapters Nine and Ten.

Figure 8-1   Symmetrical Triangle in an Uptrend

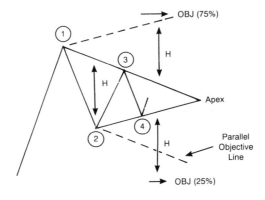

Figure 8-2   Symmetrical Triangle in a Downtrend

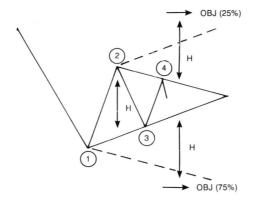

Notes to Figures 8-1 and 8-2:

1. Reversal point 1 in a Triangle in a bull market is always found at a price high.

2. Reversal point 1 in a Triangle in a bear market is always found at a price low.

3. "H" is the primary method of obtaining a "height" measuring objective.

4. The dashed lines are parallel objective lines. This is a secondary method of obtaining a measuring objective.

I. **Characteristics of a Symmetrical Triangle**

    A. Directional tendencies

        1. Continuation—75%

        2. Reversal—25%

    B. Measuring objectives

        1. Height of Triangle at point 2, or

        2. Parallel objective line

    C. Optimum breakout time period: No more than three-quarters of the horizontal distance from point 1 to the apex

    D. Volume considerations

        1. Irregularly lower during formation

        2. Should increase on upside breakout

    E. Open interest considerations (futures)

        1. Rising (ideally) prior to reaching objective

        2. If declines past objective, exit

II. **Options Strategies Prior to Breakout**

    A. Check implied volatility

        1. With respect to recent history

        2. Likelihood of increase/decrease

    B. Buying straddles

        1. Both legs at-the-money (delta neutral)

        2. Directional breakout leg in-the-money

    C. Ratio backspreads

        1. Delta neutral

        2. Aggressively directional

III. **Options Strategies at the Breakout and Pullback (if any)**

    A. Obtain a volume estimate during breakout trading session

    B. Check actual breakout volume when available

    C. Drop one-half of losing leg on valid breakout

    D. Remove remaining one-half losing leg on pullback

IV. Options Strategies at Objective

    A. Take partial profits and enter trailing stop (based on chart of underlying instrument)

    B. If underlying instrument is a futures contract, check open interest for signs of profit taking by the "smart money"; if down, exit

CHAPTER 9

SYMMETRICAL TRIANGLE IN AN UPTREND

LONG STRADDLE

Options Strategy	When to Use	Technical Situation
Long Straddle	Immediate move expected	Within Symmetrical Triangle

A long straddle is composed of a long call and long put with the same strike and expiration. This allows the holder of a long straddle to realize substantial profits if the market moves far enough in *either* direction. The technical aspects of the Symmetrical Triangle formation (Chapter Eight) strongly suggest that a long straddle be used as a starting point to investigate "leading-off" on this pattern.

This chapter will develop the important properties of a long options straddle and monitor the outcome of a long straddle position to trade a possible Symmetrical Triangle formation.

June '87 Japanese Yen Case Study

On the June '87 Japanese Yen futures chart in Figure 9-1, prices are in an uptrend as a Symmetrical Triangle pattern formed. The International Monetary Market (IMM) in Chicago quotes currency futures in U.S. terms (Dollars per unit of foreign currency). Reversal point 1 in the Triangle is the highest price in the pattern, as it should be in an uptrending market. All other things being equal, an upside breakout is expected with a probability of 75 percent.

But the other IMM foreign exchange futures charts (not shown) contain ominous-looking potential Head & Shoulders Top patterns. This reduces the probability of an upside breakout on the Yen chart to more of a fifty-fifty proposition. A significant price move from the Triangle breakout (in either direction) is expected. Thus, use of a nondirectional (delta-neutral) at-the-money long straddle will be investigated.

To make any long straddle position flexible for follow-up action, a minimum of two options contracts on each leg of the straddle is suggested. This will allow for lifting one-half of the losing leg at the breakout and lifting the remaining one-half if a pullback occurs. An overview of the situation is:

Given

1. There has been a sustained bull market in most major currencies with respect to the U.S. Dollar.

2. Possible Head & Shoulders Tops are developing on the IMM currency futures charts of the D-Mark, Swiss Franc and British Pound; necklines have not yet been broken to the downside.

3. Volume and open interest are acting in classic fashion during the current consolidation in the Yen; see Figure 9-1.

4. Four reversals of the minor trend allow converging Symmetrical Triangle boundary lines to be drawn as of the close Tuesday, May 12, 1987.

5. The height of the Triangle as measured at reversal point 2 is 160 points. This will be applied to the breakout price to obtain an objective.

6. Calculation of the latest date that a breakout could occur and not be beyond the optimum breakout period (defined as three-quarters of the distance from point 1 to the apex):

   • Point 1 = Monday, April 27

   • Apex = Thursday, May 21

   • Total distance = 19 trading days

   • 3/4 x 19 = 14 1/4 trading days

   • April 27 + 14 trading days = close Thursday, May 14—
     this is two trading days from "now"

7. Conservative measuring objectives (assuming breakout does not occur until Thursday, May 14):

   • Upside: .7228 + 160 points = .7388

   • Downside: .7168 - 160 points = .7008

Statistics

1. Date: Tuesday, May 12th

2. June options last trading day: June 5 (23 calendar days)

3. June futures close = .7172

4. .7200 call delta = .45

5. .7200 put delta = -.55

6. Implied volatility (average of put and call) = 11.0%

7. One tick in both the Yen futures (.0001) and options (.01) = 12.50 $US

8. Options prices for close May 12, 1987 were:

JAPANESE YEN (IMM) 12,500,000 yen; cents per 100 yen

Strike	Calls–Settle			Puts–Settle		
Price	Jun-c	Jly-c	Aug-c	Jun-p	Jly-p	Aug-p
70	2.02	2.77	....	0.29	0.44	....
71	1.30	2.05	....	0.57	0.70	....
72	0.74	1.44	....	1.03	1.07	....
73	0.40	0.97	....	1.67	1.60	....
74	0.23	0.64	....	2.50	....	....
75	0.11	0.42	....	3.37	....	....

Est. vol. 12,437, Mon vol. 1,540 calls, 6,579 puts
Open interest Mon; 42,989 calls, 91,756 puts

Figure 9-1   Symmetrical Triangle

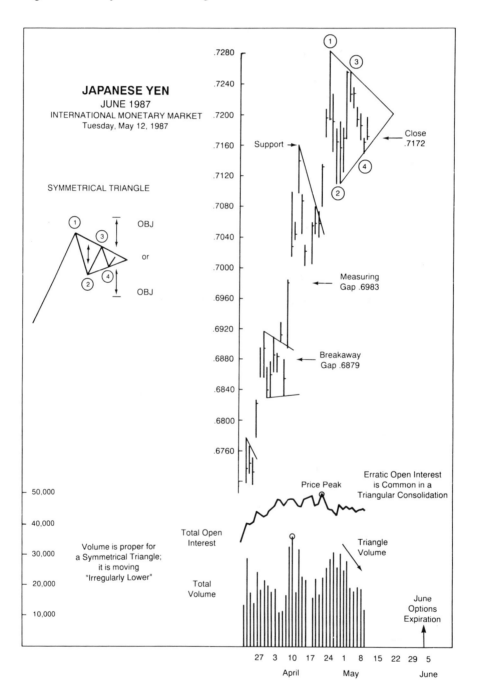

JAPANESE YEN
JUNE 1987
INTERNATIONAL MONETARY MARKET
Tuesday, May 12, 1987

SYMMETRICAL TRIANGLE

Support →
Close .7172

Measuring Gap .6983

Breakaway Gap .6879

Erratic Open Interest is Common in a Triangular Consolidation

Price Peak

Total Open Interest

Volume is proper for a Symmetrical Triangle; it is moving "Irregularly Lower"

Total Volume

Triangle Volume

June Options Expiration

27 3 10 17 24 1 8 15 22 29 5
April   May   June

VOLATILITY PREMIUMS

Markets focus on important fundamental reports. The logical expectation is that a substantial price move may occur following the release of new fundamental news. This leads to the simplistic trading approach of buying options.

But options premiums, due to the effect of implied volatility, often increase as a well-publicized release date approaches. Obviously a trader does not want to pay too much if a trading strategy requires purchase of options. Thus, a look at a chart of recent (last three months) daily postings of implied volatility is, at minimum, necessary to make an intelligent assessment of of volatility premiums.

The optimum situation occurs when the technician locates a Triangle formation on a price chart at least a week prior to the release of a market-sensitive economic report. An early price breakout may take place because of an unexpected event totally unrelated to the fundamental figure on which market participants will be keying. A double-barreled effect favors the trader who is long premium: an increase in volatility plus a directional price move.

A situation that could easily transpire when a market is waiting for an important and well-advertised piece of news is shown in Figure 9-2. Note the rather extreme and inverse relationship between historical and implied volatility. The most frustrating predicament an options trader faces is to be correct on market direction but lose money because of a drop in implied volatility when holding long positions.

Figure 9-2   Hypothetical Volatility Interaction

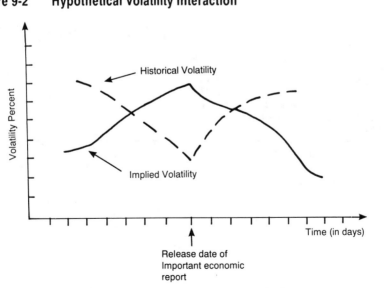

TRADING PLAN

A long straddle using the closest-to-the-money put and call will be monitored. Specifically:

Buy one June 72 call at	.74	=	925.00 $US
Buy one June 72 put at	1.03	=	1,287.50
	1.77	=	2,212.50 $US (per one-lot)

The implied volatility chart (puts and calls combined) must be examined. Figure 9-3 shows that the 11 percent implied volatility on the at-the-money Yen futures options on May 12 is slightly higher than average over the last three months. Although this is not the ideal situation, at least implied volatility is lower than the 13 1/2 percent that was recorded on two previous occasions in April.

The risk/reward diagram for the long June 72 Yen straddle is contained in Figure 9-4. The conservative measuring objectives, both to the upside and

Figure 9-3   Implied Volatility of Japanese Yen Calls and Puts

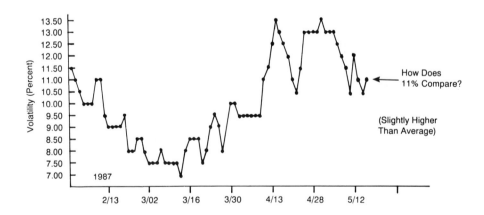

downside, are indicated. When this graphic analysis is first examined, it appears that the reward-to-risk relationship is extremely poor. The downside objective, for instance, would produce a .7023 - .7008 = 15 point profit. Yet a maximum risk of 177 points is present in the unlikely event that the June Yen future was exactly at the 72 strike when both options expired. The potential upside reward seen in Figure 9-4 is even worse—only 11 points!

On the surface, every potential Triangle pattern traded with a long straddle will produce an apparently unsuitable risk/reward relationship. But remember, the initial position will not be held until expiration. Something will happen on the price chart. Quotes will either move too far into the apex of the formation or a breakout will occur. In either case, follow-up action will remove or modify the original long straddle.

Figure 9-4   Long 72 Straddle: Risk/Reward Diagram at Expiration

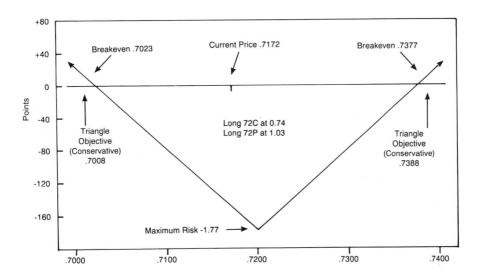

DELTA POSITION

To determine whether this position is truly nondirectional when first established, the deltas of the individual options must be known. In this case, the long call has a delta of +.45 and the long put has a delta of -.55.

A one-lot (contract) spread would produce a delta position of: +.45 - .55 = -.10. This is a slightly bearish initial position. But it is close enough to delta neutral (0) for a small trader.

A more exacting position would involve long 11 calls and long 9 puts.

Long 11 calls	=	+ .45 x 11	=	+4.95
Long 9 puts	=	- .55 x 9	=	-4.95
				0.00 Delta

If this exact delta-neutral spread was used, a very small price move in either direction would produce similar results. As prices move out of the Triangle, the spread would automatically assume the proper directional bias. If no follow-up action were taken, an upside breakout would be more profitable in the long run. The excess two long calls would create a position that would move toward a delta of +11.0 given a substantial price rally.

In this case study a 2 X 2 long straddle will be monitored.

BREAKOUT: REMOVE ONE-HALF OF LOSING LEG

A downside breakout took place on Wednesday, May 13 with a close of .7151 on the June Yen (Figure 9-5). From the breakout level of .7164, the height distance (H) of 160 points is subtracted to create a downside measuring objective of .7004 on the June Yen chart. An aggressive strategy dictates removing one-half of the losing (long call) leg. The calculations that follow are based on closing prices for May 13.

Sell one June 72 call at .60
(for a loss of .74 - .60 = .14)

Present Position

Long two June 72 puts
(open trade profit .06 x 2)
Long one June 72 call
(open trade loss .14)
Delta = - .583 + - .583 + .416 = - .75

Figure 9-5   Triangle Breakout

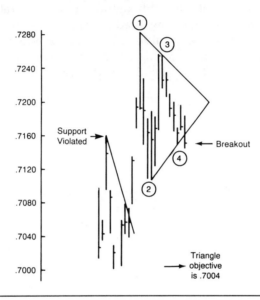

JAPANESE YEN
JUNE 1987
INTERNATIONAL MONETARY MARKET
Wednesday, May 13, 1987

U.S. trade deficit figures are to be released the following trading session (ten minutes after the 7:20 AM Chicago open). Implied volatility remains high as traders are expecting a significant price move following the release of this important fundamental statistic.

PULLBACK: REMOVE REMAINING LOSING LEG

The next trading session, Thursday, May 14, a pullback (price rally) into the Triangle took place (Figure 9-6). This dictated the removal of the other one-half of the losing (long call) leg. The volume on the reaction was lower than the breakout volume (17,521 versus 18,870). In addition, open interest expanded on the downside breakout and declined on the pullback rally. These are both bearish signals for a futures technician.

Sell one June 72 call at .71
(for a loss of .74 - .71 = .03)

Present Position

Long two June 72 puts
(open trade loss .25 X 2)
Delta = -.51 x 2 = -1.02

It is interesting to note that although the Yen future rallied in price to above the level at which the long straddle was placed, the remaining call option was liquidated at a small loss. This was due to a combination of factors. A slight premium decay occurred because of the passage of time, and, more likely, implied volatility declined after the report came out.

Figure 9-6   Pullback into Triangle

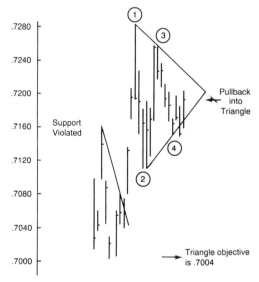

JAPANESE YEN SYMMETRICAL TRIANGLE OUTCOME

On Tuesday, May 26 (following the three-day Memorial Day weekend holiday in the U.S.), the downside objective of .7004 was met. This is illustrated in Figure 9-7.

Something technical was also occurring that is not apparent on the chart. Moving average models suggested that fund managers using this technique

Figure 9-7   Symmetrical Triangle Measuring Objective Met

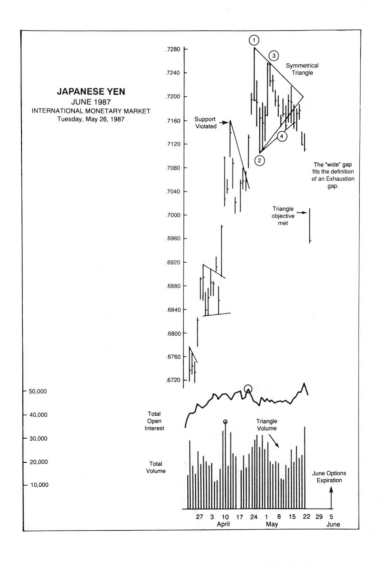

would be heavy short sellers on the close. This would establish new short positions for them. A knee-jerk reaction to the upside often follows these computer-based sell programs.

Adding the fact that the "wide" gap on the Yen chart could easily be an Exhaustion Gap—which is typically quickly filled—a technician would remove all bearish positions. The long two puts brought 253 points each as of the close on May 26.

RECAP

Using the closing prices for May 26:

Initial cost of 2 x 2 straddle	=	1.77 x 2	=	-3.54
Sell (liquidate) first call at .60	=			+ .60
Sell (liquidate) second call at .71	=			+. 71
Sell (liquidate) two puts at 2.53	=	2.53 x 2	=	+5.06
Result	=			+2.83

283 points x 12.50 $US/point = 3,537.50 $US (before commissions)

RESULTS OF HOLDING INITIAL STRADDLE

In summarizing this case study, a trader should judiciously examine the results of holding the initial straddle until the close on May 26. This assumes no follow-up action was undertaken. The values of the legs of the straddle on May 26 were:

June 72 call	=	.09
June 72 put	=	2.53
Straddle	=	2.62

The straddle was placed initially at a debit of 1.77 points (1 X 1). Thus a gross profit of (2.62 - 1.77) X 2 = 1.70 was realized for each 2 X 2 spread. The more aggressive trader, reacting to unfolding technical events, generated superior results—grossing 283 points versus the static 170-point trade.

A final observation: When any long straddle is held until a Triangle objective is met and then liquidated, the results are better than the original risk/reward diagram indicates. This is because a time premium still exists in the profitable leg—beyond the intrinsic value. The option price of the losing leg has not declined to zero, so a time premium is also present here as well. The risk/reward diagram correctly assumes that the straddle is trading at the intrinsic values of each leg at expiration.

To satisfy curiosity as to what occurred on the Yen chart after the Triangle objective was met, Figure 9-8 shows the price activity through the expiration of the June option series. A violent price reaction to the upside occurred. A trader trying to maintain a bearish view would have been forced out of any remaining positions.

Figure 9-8   June Yen Chart at Options Expiration

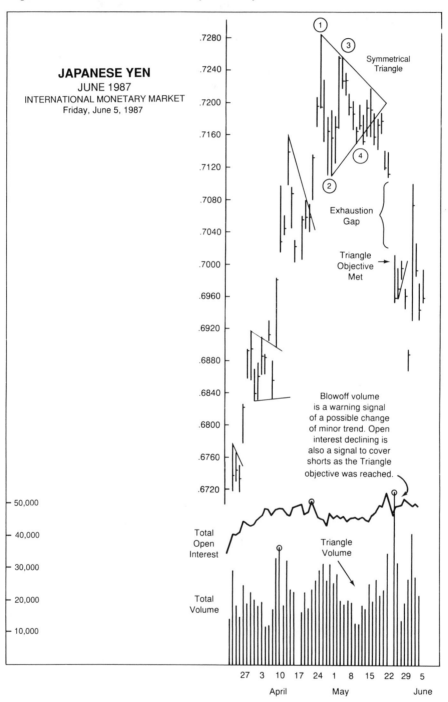

JAPANESE YEN
JUNE 1987
INTERNATIONAL MONETARY MARKET
Friday, June 5, 1987

Symmetrical
Triangle

Exhaustion
Gap

Triangle
Objective
Met

Blowoff volume
is a warning signal
of a possible change
of minor trend. Open
interest declining is
also a signal to cover
shorts as the Triangle
objective was reached.

Total
Open
Interest

Triangle
Volume

Total
Volume

CHAPTER **10**

POSSIBLE SYMMETRICAL
TRIANGLE IN A DOWNTREND

PUT RATIO BACKSPREAD

Options Strategy	When to Use	Technical Situation
Put Ratio Backspread	Greater probability market will move to downside	Within Symmetrical Triangle in a bear market

The probability of a Symmetrical Triangle price pattern acting as a continuation pattern is approximately 75 percent. This means that in three out of four cases the Triangle breakout will be in the same direction as the price move into the Triangle. In this chapter, an options trader will use the higher probability direction to skew or modify a position taken within the Triangle toward realizing greater reward if the breakout is in the expected direction. A ratio backspread options strategy has the desired risk/reward diagram.

- A *ratio spread* is an options spread in which the number of long options is unequal to the number of short options.

- A *backspread* is an option spread in which more options are purchased than sold short.

June '87 Eurodollar Case Study

The Eurodollar Time Deposit chart in Figure 10-1 clearly exhibits a price downtrend. Short-term (three months) U.S. dollar interest rates have been increasing. Three clear-cut reversals of the minor price trend are in place on the chart. Additional technical factors are:

Given

1. The price high today, April 22, 1987, is 92.92 and could be the fourth reversal. A lower high the next trading session is needed to construct the official boundary lines of a Symmetrical Triangle.

2. Reversal point 2 (in Figure 10-1) is actually composed of the two daily price highs at 93.05 and 93.01. The height of the Triangle will be measured from the 93.05 high.

3. If the upper boundary line of the Triangle does form, the line will begin at the 93.01 price high. The line will thus be constructed without cutting through any price activity when first drawn. This is a most basic rule for all classical bar chartists.

4. Today's price activity consisted of a higher high (than yesterday) followed by a lower settlement price. Assuming today's high of 92.92 is the fourth reversal point in the Triangle:

    • Approximate breakout levels are:
       Downside: 92.70
       Upside: 92.85

    • Height of triangle = 41 basis points (ticks)
       One tick = .01 = 25$ US
       Downside objective = 92.70 - .41 = 92.29
       Upside objective = 92.85 + .41 = 93.26

5. If 92.92 is reversal point four, the breakout should occur by Friday (in two days).

6. A U.S. GNP figure is due out tomorrow morning (ten minutes after the IMM opening).

Statistics

1. Date: Wednesday, April 22, 1987

2. June option last trading day: June 15, 1987 (55 days)

3. June futures close: 92.80

Figure 10-1   Possible Symmetrical Triangle Forming

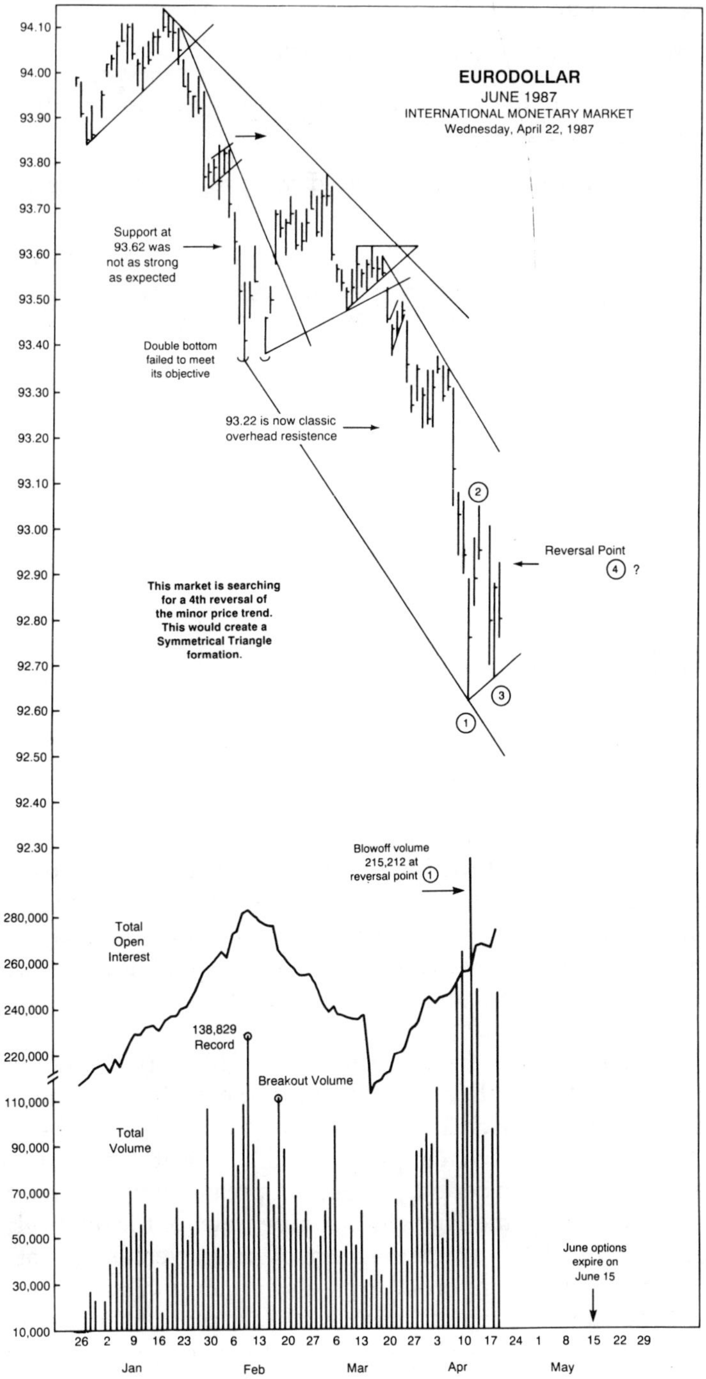

EURODOLLAR
JUNE 1987
INTERNATIONAL MONETARY MARKET
Wednesday, April 22, 1987

Support at
93.62 was
not as strong
as expected

Double bottom
failed to meet
its objective

93.22 is now classic
overhead resistance

Reversal Point
④ ?

This market is searching
for a 4th reversal of
the minor price trend.
This would create a
Symmetrical Triangle
formation.

Blowoff volume
215,212 at
reversal point ①

Total
Open
Interest

138,829
Record

Breakout Volume

Total
Volume

June options
expire on
June 15

4. 92.75 put delta = -.47

5. 93.00 put delta = -.67

6. Average put implied volatility = 17.4%

7. One tick in both the Eurodollar futures and options = .01 = one basis point = 25 $US

8. Options prices on close Wednesday, April 22, 1987 were:

EURODOLLAR (CME) $ million; pts. of 100%

Strike Price	Calls—Settle			Puts—Settle		
	Jun-c	Sep-c	Dec-c	Jun-p	Sep-p	Dec-p
9225	....	....	....	0.04	0.34	0.60
9250	0.39	0.38	0.44	0.09	0.45	0.72
9275	0.22	0.27	0.33	0.17	0.58	0.84
9300	0.11	0.19	0.26	0.31	0.74	1.01
9325	0.04	0.12	0.19	0.49	0.92	1.18
9350	0.01	0.08	0.13	0.70	1.12	1.36

Est. vol. 19,723, Tues vol. 8,383 calls, 15,707 puts
Open interest Tues;71,052 calls, 116,610 puts

TRADING PLAN

An options trader wanting to lead off on the possible formation of a Triangle in a bear market would create a position with limited upside reward and unlimited downside reward. Note that a profit would be generated given a big price move in *either* direction. The unlimited gain, however, would accrue in the direction of the high probability breakout (downward). The put ratio backspread has the desired risk/reward characteristics.

Profit potential on an upside breakout (25 percent probability) is limited to the net credit taken in when the position was initiated. The downside potential (75 percent probability), however, is unlimited in a collapsing market.

Because more options are purchased than sold short, the trader is "long premium." A chart of implied volatility must be examined to determine that the options are not too rich in price. The chart of the closest-to-the-money puts in Figure 10-2 shows that implied volatility is relatively high compared to the recent three-month period. The option spreader will need the expected price movement out of the Triangle to compensate for the relatively expensive options. The risk/reward diagram of profit versus loss at various expiration prices will be important to assess the merits of this trade. A matrix of various outcomes is found in Table 10-1. A plot of these outcomes is illustrated in the traditional shape of a put ratio backspread in Figure 10-3.

Figure 10-2   Implied Volatility—Eurodollar Future Puts

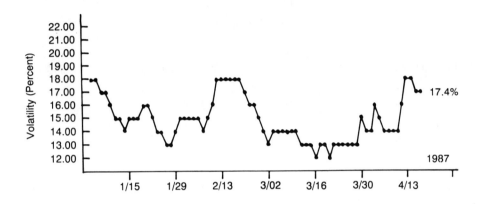

Put Ratio Backspread (Delta-Neutral)

Long three 92.75 June puts
-47 x 3 = 141 bearish deltas

Short two 93.00 June puts
67 x 2 = 134 bullish deltas

Net = short 7 deltas

June futures
close on
Wednesday,
April 22
= 92.80

Some traders remove the decimal point and refer to a delta of -.07 as being short seven deltas. It does not matter what convention is used as long as everyone knows it and it is consistent. In this book, the decimal point in a delta position will be shown. The delta of -.07 is equivalent in risk (for a small price move) to a short position of .07 of one Eurodollar futures contract.

Cost of Position

Long three 92.75 June puts at .17 x 3   =   .51 debit
Short two 93.00 June puts at .31 x 2   =   .62 credit
Net =   11-tick credit   11 x 25$ =   275$US

Table 10-1   Tabular Risk/Reward at Expiration

Put Ratio Backspread

Long three 92.75 puts
Short two 93.00 puts

Price at Expiration	92.00	92.25	92.50	92.75	93.00	93.25
Long 3 92.75 puts	+2.25	+1.50	+ .75	0	0	0
Short 2 93.00 puts	-2.00	-1.50	-1.00	- .50	0	0
Spread result	+ .25	0	- .25	- .50	0	0
.11 Initial credit	+ .11	+ .11	+ .11	+ .11	+ .11	+ .11
Net result	+ .36	+ .11	- .14	- .39	+ .11	+ .11

Figure 10-3   Risk/Reward Diagram at Expiration

Put Ratio Backspread

Long three 92.75 puts
Short two 93.00 puts

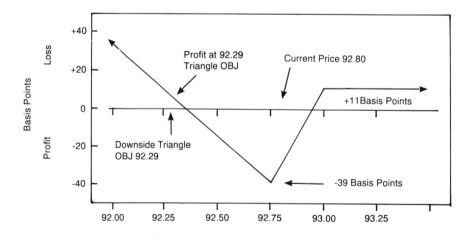

BREAKOUT: REMOVE ONE-HALF OF LOSING LEG

On Friday, April 24, 1987, the June Eurodollars settled at 92.60, out the downside of the Triangle. This can be seen in Figure 10-4. An aggressive trader would remove one-half of the losing leg in the put ratio backspread. The calculations that follow are based on closing prices for April 24.

Buy one 93.00 June put at .44
(for a loss of .31 - .44 = .13)

Present Position

Short one 93.00 June put
(open trade loss .13)

Long three 92.75 June puts
(open trade profit .09 X 3)

Delta = -(-.81) + 3(-.63) = -1.08

Figure 10-4   Triangle Breakout

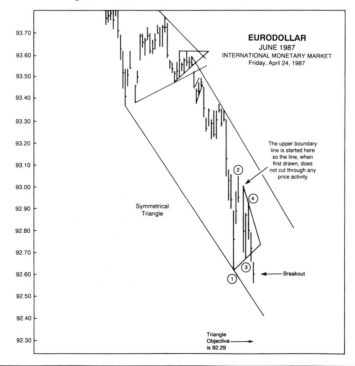

PULLBACK: REMOVE REMAINING LOSING LEG

On Wednesday, April 29, 1987, a pullback to the Triangle took place. The daily high in Figure 10-5 was up to the apex of the Triangle. This does not destroy the formation. Aggressive traders would now remove the remaining one-half of the losing leg.

Buy one 93.00 June put at .42
(for a loss of .31 - .42 = .11)

Present Position

Long three 92.75 June puts
(open trade profit .07 X 3)

Delta of new position = 3(-.66) = -1.98

Figure 10-5   Pullback to Triangle

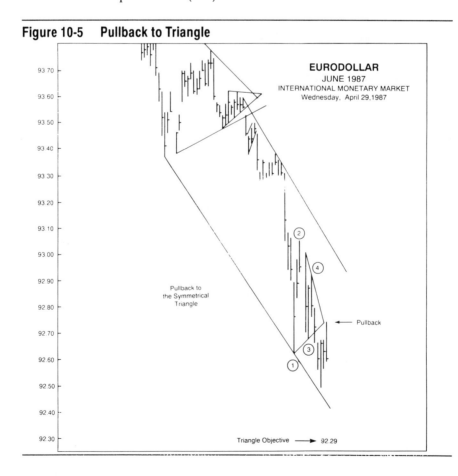

EURODOLLAR
JUNE 1987
INTERNATIONAL MONETARY MARKET
Wednesday, April 29,1987

Pullback to
the Symmetrical
Triangle

←— Pullback

Triangle Objective ——▶ 92.29

EURODOLLAR TRIANGLE OUTCOME

The sequence of events that led to the removal of all the remaining puts is shown in Figure 10-6. Tuesday, May 5, 1987 was an Inside Range Day. This is a minor trend change indicator. Because prices were in a selloff going into this trading session, a bounce to the upside would be expected the next trading session.

The minimum objective of the Inside Range Day is to exceed that day's high of 92.47. Overhead resistance is found at the April 27 low of 92.49.

If trading outright (unlimited risk) short positions, protective buy-stop orders would be lowered to 92.51, just above the resistance. Options traders would consider exiting from the bearish position on the first *close* (note the staying power of options) above 92.49. This occurred May 7 when the June Eurodollars settled at 92.57.

Figure 10-6   Symmetrical Triangle Outcome

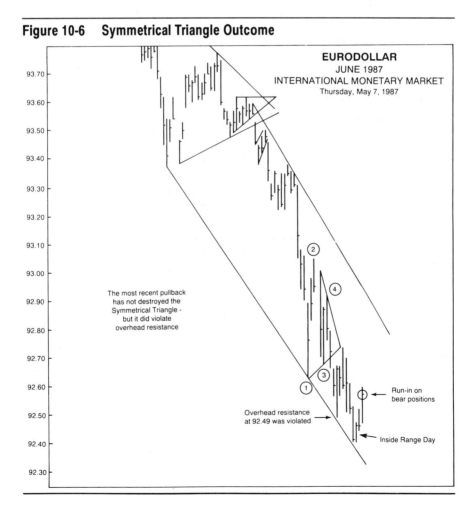

Therefore:

Sell three 92.75 June puts at .26 X 3 = .78 credit

Overall Result

Long three 92.75 June puts at	.51	debit	
Exit credit =	.78		
	.27	credit	
Short one 93.00 June put at	.31	credit	
Exit debit =	.44		(Breakout)
	.13	debit	
Short one 93.00 June put at	.31	credit	
Exit debit =	.42		(Pullback)
	.11	debit	

.27 - .13 - .11 = + .03 (profit before commissions)

OUTCOME ASSUMING ORIGINAL 3 X 2 PUT RATIO BACKSPREAD STILL ON

Examine the results of holding the initial 3 X 2 ratio backspread. This assumes no follow-up action was taken on the breakout or pullback. As before, the position was unwound on the close May 7 after the Inside Range Day and subsequent violation of overhead resistance.

Sell three 92.75 June puts at .26 x 3	=	.78 credit
Buy two 93.00 June puts at .45 x 2	=	.90 debit
Net debit	=	.12

Result

Initial credit	=	.11	
Ending debit	=	.12	
	=	.01	loss before commisions

This was a slightly worse outcome than the active traders' results in which they made their position more aggressively bearish at the breakout and pullback to the Triangle.

MORE AGGRESSIVE STRATEGY (Not Delta-Neutral)

Creating a put ratio backspread with a delta negative initial bias would be a more aggressive strategy. Numerous option strikes are available to shift the risk/reward diagram to the left or right and produce very aggressive initial delta positions. In this example, the same two 92.75 and 93.00 strikes will be used, but the ratio will be changed. The risk/reward diagram in Figure 10-7 shows that a downside breakout of the Triangle must occur for the strategy to produce profits. Even a large price move to the upside would generate a three-tick loss unless follow-up action is taken if an upside breakout is posted.

Long two 92.75 puts at .17 X 2 = .34 debit
Delta = -.47

Short one 93.00 put at .31 credit
Delta = .67

Net debit = .03 = 75$US
Delta of position = (-.47 X 2) + .67 = -.27

Figure 10-7   Risk/Reward Diagram at Expiration

Put Ratio Backspread

Long two 92.75 puts
Short one 93.00 puts

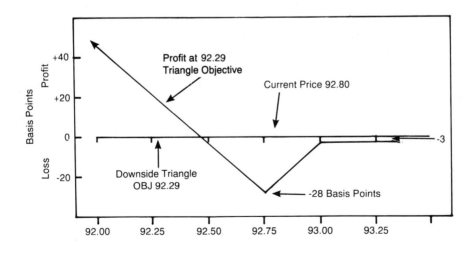

Unwind When Resistance Penetrated

The results stated below assume no follow-up action. The entire 2 X 1 put ratio backspread was removed on May 7 as before, when overhead resistance was penetrated.

Buy one 93.00 put at .45	=	.45 debit
Sell two 92.75 puts at .26 x 2	=	.52 credit
		.07 credit

Result

Initial debit	=	.03
Ending credit	=	.07
		.04 profit before commisions

A four-tick profit was realized. An active trader, reacting to subsequent market conditions, would have produced a greater profit by unlegging the spread.

POSTSCRIPT

Figure 10-8 shows that the Symmetrical Triangle on the June '87 Eurodollar chart did eventually achieve its measuring objective of 92.30. But the second pullback to the Triangle was so severe that conservative traders were forced off a bearish stance. This was done so that a winning trade would not be turned into a loser.

A schematic overview of the technical aspects of this case study is included in Figure 10-9.

Figure 10-8   Triangle Objective Eventually Met

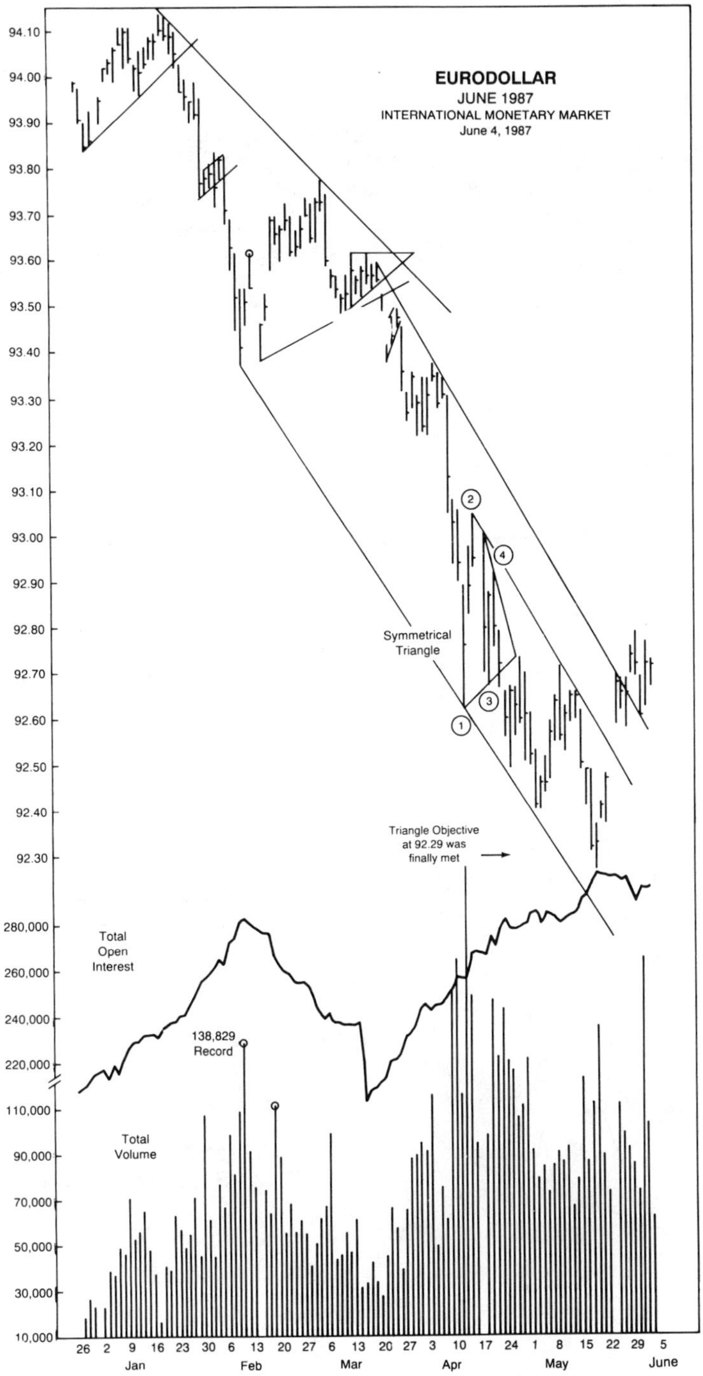

EURODOLLAR
JUNE 1987
INTERNATIONAL MONETARY MARKET
June 4, 1987

Symmetrical
Triangle

Triangle Objective
at 92.29 was
finally met

Total
Open
Interest

138,829
Record

Total
Volume

Figure 10-9   Schematic Overview of the Triangle and Its Outcome

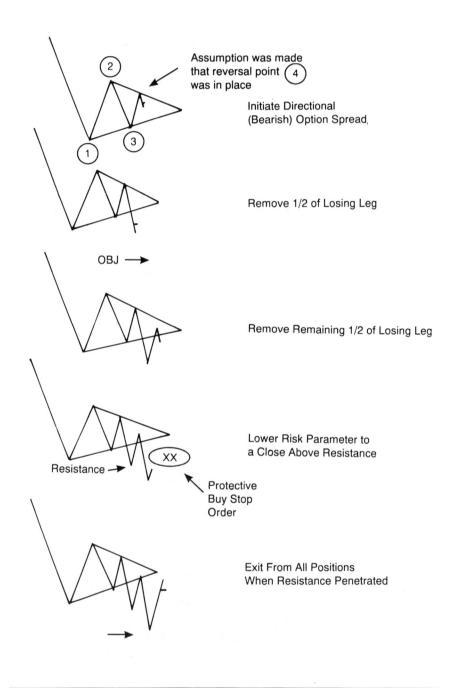

CHAPTER 11

TRENDLINE TEST

LONG STRADDLE

Options Strategy	When to Use	Technical Situation
Long Straddle	Immediate move expected	Testing a trendline

Only two points are necessary to draw a straight line. Trendlines are constructed by a line drawn tangent to reversals of the minor trend at two price highs or two price lows. When first constructed, a trendline should not cut through any intervening price activity.

An up trendline is the straight line that connects at least two price lows on a chart. This is illustrated in Figure 11-1. A line constructed parallel to the trendline beginning at the intervening price high is referred to as a parallel return line. This line can serve as a reasonable expectation of the extent of the next price move in the same direction as the prevailing trend.

Simply breaking a trendline with a close beyond it does not produce an automatic measuring objective. In the absence of any classical bar charting price pattern, the height of the possible channel may provide a clue as to the possible magnitude of the price move beyond the trendline.

September '87 Swiss Franc Case Study

The down-sloping trendline on the Swiss Franc futures chart in Figure 11-2 is composed of three points. Any trendline becomes significant when a third "touch" of the line occurs. When prices again approach an important trendline, it can imply either:

- a low-risk entry for new positions in the direction of the major trend, or

- an impending breakout and reversal of the major trend

To determine which scenario will occur, traders should assume that the trend will continue until the trendline is decisively penetrated. If it is broken, a substantial price move is likely to occur.

The September 1987 Swiss Franc chart can be used to determine whether a long straddle might be appropriate when an important trendline is tested.

Given

1. A Reversal Day was posted Monday, July 27, 1987. This is a higher price high followed by a lower close. It is typically a sign of a reversal of the minor trend.

2. The daily high on the Reversal Day tested the three-point down trendline on the September '87 Swiss chart.

3. The September Swiss Franc future settled at .6523.

Figure 11-1

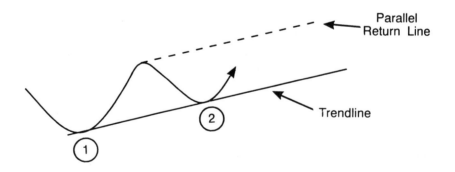

4. One tick in both the Swiss Franc futures and options = 12.50 $US.

5. Options prices for the close July 27 were:

SWISS FRANC (IMM) 125,000 francs; cents per franc

Strike	Calls—Settle			Puts—Settle		
Price	Aug-c	Sep-c	Oct-c	Aug-p	Sep-p	Oct-p
63	....	2.38	....	0.01	0.16	0.26
64	1.29	1.58	....	0.06	0.36	0.48
65	0.50	0.94	1.59	0.27	0.71	0.80
66	0.14	0.50	1.08	0.90	1.28	1.25
67	0.03	0.25	0.70	1.75	2.01	....
68	0.01	0.12	0.43	2.77	2.86	....

Est. vol. 1,446; Fri vol. 1,001 calls, 1,583 puts
Open interest Fri; 25,837 calls, 25,283 puts

Figure 11-2   Testing a Three-Point Trendline

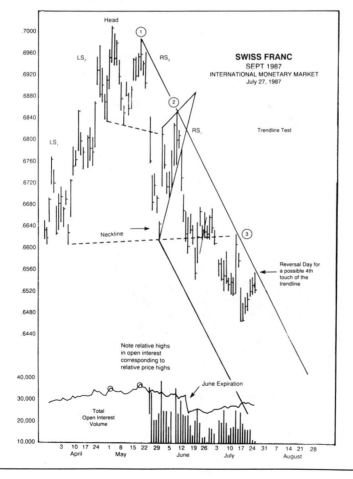

Trading Plan

The technical assumption is that prices will move significantly away (in either direction) from the three-point trendline.

The closest-to-the-money strike is the .6500. The September expiration series will be used for liquidity considerations and because the nearby August options expire in only 11 days. A one-lot long straddle would cost:

Buy one Sept 65 call at	.94	=	1175.00$US
Buy one Sept 65 put at	.71	=	887.50
	1.65		2062.50$US

This simplistic strategy is not delta neutral. A bullish bias exists because the call leg is in-the-money. This is one of the problems that will be addressed in the outcome of this strategy.

FOLLOW-UP

In Figure 11-3, technicians will notice that four days of sideways activity (including Inside and Outside Range Days) followed the initiation of the long straddle. This is the opposite of what was expected and desired. Patience finally paid off as the major downtrend continued.

The next problem is when and where to remove the long straddle. In the case of the September '87 Swiss chart, a simple strategy of staying with the position until a higher price high (than the previous trading session) will be tested. This suggests removing the straddle on the close Wednesday, August 12, 1987. The options prices that day were:

SWISS FRANC (IMM) 125,000 francs; cents per franc

Strike	Calls—Settle			Puts—Settle		
Price	Sep-c	Oct-c	Dec-c	Sep-p	Oct-p	Dec-p
62	1.87	....	....	0.13	0.31	0.73
63	1.08	1.78	2.29	0.34	0.57	1.05
64	0.52	1.18	1.70	0.77	0.95	1.46
65	0.22	0.74	1.26	1.47	1.49	1.98
66	0.08	0.45	0.91	2.32	2.18	2.62
67	0.03	0.26	0.65	3.28	....	3.33

Est. vol. 2,129, Tues vol. 2,537 calls, 1,511 puts
Open interest Tues; 26,934 calls, 25,647 puts

Outcome

Sell one Sept 65 call at	.22	=	275.00 $US
Sell one Sept 65 put at	1.47	=	1,837.50
	1.69		2,112.50 $US

The net result of this trade was not very exciting—a four-tick gain. The $50 per one-lot straddle profit would barely have covered commissions. Additional considerations should have been addressed:

1. The evenly balanced position (in the ratio of 1:1) had an initial bullish bias. A delta-neutral strategy would have produced better results given that the profitable direction was a bearish price move.

2. A chart of implied volatility should have been consulted. If implied volatility was unusually high, a long premium strategy would not have been desirable.

3. Aggressive traders will note that no follow-up action was taken. Students observing the price down move away from the trendline would have been quick to suggest that the losing long call leg be reduced.

ANOTHER TRENDLINE TEST

Another test of the (now four-point) trendline took place on the rally, August 14. This can be seen in Figure 11-4. Although the intraday high on the daily bar chart was above the down-sloping trendline, the *close* was not. Thus, the line is still being tested. The September futures settled at .6425. The prevailing options prices were:

SWISS FRANC (IMM) 125,000 francs; cents per franc

Strike Price	Calls—Settle			Puts—Settle		
	Sep-c	Oct-c	Dec-c	Sep-p	Oct-p	Dec-p
62	2.30	....	....	0.07	0.23	0.57
63	1.43	2.13	2.57	0.19	0.42	0.90
64	0.75	1.45	1.97	0.50	0.73	1.23
65	0.33	0.93	1.45	1.07	1.20	1.72
66	0.13	0.56	1.06	1.88	1.82	2.30
67	0.08	0.33	0.74	2.78	....	2.97

Est. vol. 2,487, Thur vol. 2,787 calls, 1,492 puts
Open interest Thur; 27,481 calls, 26,523 puts

Figure 11-3   Outcome of Trendline Test

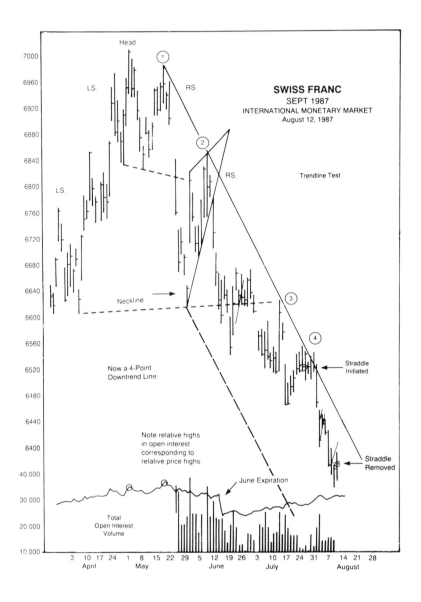

A similar naive strategy of purchasing the closest-to-the-money puts and calls will be investigated. This was the .6400 strike:

Buy one Sept 64 call at	.75	=	937.50$US
Buy one Sept 64 put at	.50	=	625.00
	1.25		1,562.50$US

Figure 11-4   Another Trendline Test

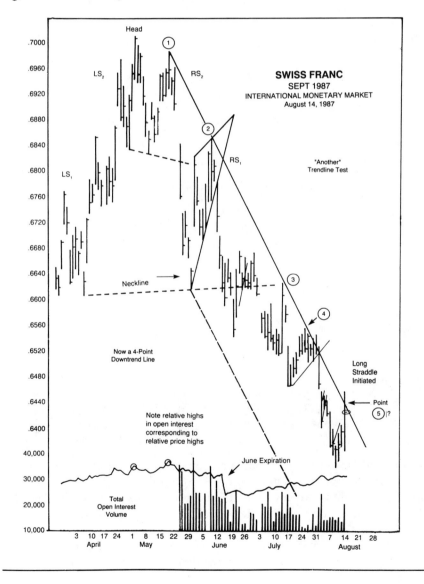

Because the call purchased is the option that is in-the-money, the delta of this long straddle is positive. The position carries an initial bullish bias. The ramifications of this are discussed in the outcome at the end of the case study.

Two trading days later, a decisive upside penetration of the major down trendline took place (Figure 11-5). One major contingent of buyers were fund managers who use moving average models to dictate their trading strategy. They were forced to cover shorts in the Swiss Franc and other IMM currency futures. The decline in open interest on the price rally confirmed this.

FOLLOW-UP

The same strategy of holding the straddle until a lower low is recorded will again be examined. This occurred on Tuesday, August 25 and can be seen in Figure 11-5. The September Swiss Franc settled at .6648. The option settlement prices were:

SWISS FRANC (IMM) 125,000 francs; cents per franc

Strike	Calls — Settle			Puts — Settle		
Price	Sep-c	Oct-c	Dec-c	Sep-p	Oct-p	Dec-p
64	2.50	3.22	3.51	0.02	0.18	0.50
65	1.57	2.38	2.79	0.09	0.34	0.77
66	0.79	1.67	2.15	0.31	0.62	1.12
67	0.29	1.09	1.62	0.82	1.03	1.56
68	0.08	0.68	1.19	1.59	....	2.10
69	0.03	0.41	0.85	2.53	....	2.74

Est. vol. 5,646, Mon vol. 3,074 calls, 2,477 puts
Open interest Mon; 32,194 calls, 27,856 puts

Outcome

Sell one Sept 64 call at	2.50	=	3,125.00 $US
Sell one Sept 64 put at	.02	=	25.00
	2.52		3,150.00 $US

This trade resulted in a gross profit of 252 - 125 = 127 ticks or 1,587.50 $US. This was obviously a much more worthwhile trade than the previous long straddle. This outcome benefited from the initial bullish bias and the subsequent dramatic bullish price move. A delta-neutral strategy would have reduced the gains.

A technical observation might be made here. Perhaps it can be expected that a bigger price move would be generated on the breaking of a trendline rather than on simply another touch of the line with prices continuing in the direction of the trend. If a technician believes this to be true, initiating a long straddle with a directional bias would make sense.

Figure 11-5   Outcome of Another Trendline Test

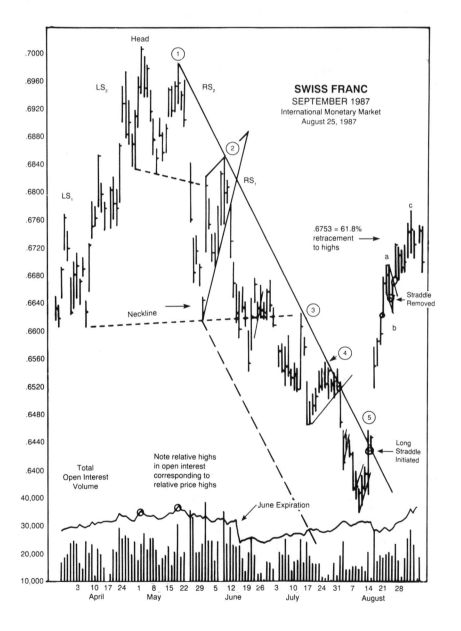

CHAPTER **12**

CONVERGING TRENDLINES

SHORT BUTTERFLY SPREAD

Options Strategy	When to Use	Technical Situation
Short Butterfly	Immediate move expected	Converging trendlines

DEFINITION

A short butterfly spread is composed of the purchase of two identical options together with the (short) sale of one option with an immediately lower strike and the (short) sale of one option with an immediately higher strike. This position is said to be "short the wings" of the butterfly.

Either all call options or all put options are used to construct a butterfly spread. The short butterfly is a credit spread. This is in keeping with the definition that any spread initiated at a credit is referred to as a short position. The maximum profit is the credit received. This occurs if the underlying market is outside the strike prices of either of the wings at expiration. At the maximum profit (credit), all the options in a short butterfly spread will be either in-the-money or out-of-the-money. This can be seen in the tabular risk/reward analysis in Table 12-1.

A butterfly spread uses three consecutive option strikes with the same expiration and type in its construction. Traditional options literature suggests that a short butterfly spread is a strategy that can be used to take advantage of an expected immediate price move when only a short time (usually a few weeks) remains until expiration. The March '89 S&P chart (Figure 12-1) showed such a prospect.

As will be discussed in conjunction with the risk/reward diagram in Figure 12-3, the maximum loss will occur if the market is exactly at the strike price of the "body" at expiration. It is a determinable maximum, equal (in points) to the difference between the strike prices of either wing and the body minus the initial credit received.

March '89 S&P 500 Case Study

Given

1. On Wednesday, March 1, 1989, the March S&Ps are testing a long-term up-sloping two-point trendline (Figure 12-1).

2. An intermediate term two-point trendline is also containing prices by sloping down from above.

3. The last trading day for the March S&P 500 futures option is March 16 (in 15 days).

    *   This is the Thursday prior to the third Friday.

    *   The option is cash settled equal to the special opening quotation on Friday.

4. One tick in both the S&P 500 futures and options = .05 = 25 $US.

5. Option prices for the close March 1, 1989 were:

S&P 500 STOCK INDEX (CME) $500 times premium

Strike	Calls–Settle			Puts–Settle		
Price	Mar-c	Apr-c	Jn-c	Mar-p	Apr-p	Jun-p
280	9.35	14.55	16.95	1.15	2.85	5.45
285	5.50	10.85	13.55	2.30	4.05	6.90
290	2.65	7.60	10.60	4.45	5.75	8.75
295	1.00	4.95	7.95	7.80	8.05	11.00
300	0.25	3.00	5.80	12.00	11.00	13.75
305	0.05	1.70	4.10	16.80	....	16.85

Est. vol. 4,279; Tues vol. 1,617 calls; 2,019 puts
Open interest Tues: 23.119 calls; 24,002 puts

Figure 12-1   Converging Two-Point Trendlines

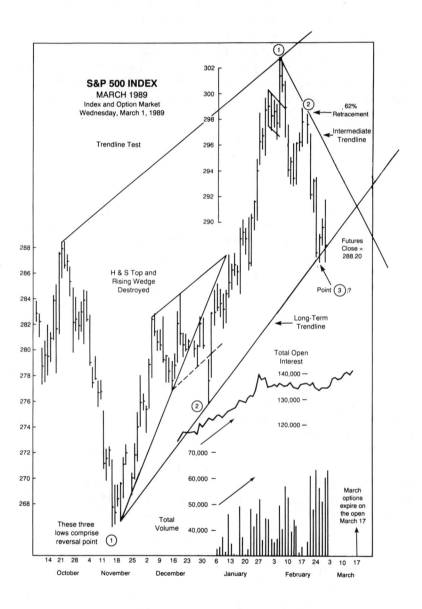

TRADING PLAN

The S&Ps are not expected to remain at the present price level. Either of the converging trendlines is expected to be violated and thus a new price move should be initiated in that direction.

The short butterfly spread is a strategy to take advantage of an immediate price move when only a few weeks remain in an option series. Therefore, the March option series will be used with 15 trading days left. The middle (long) strike price will be the closest to the current futures price.

COMMISSION CONSIDERATIONS

All of the risk/reward diagrams illustrated in this book assume zero commissions. Options traders will quickly note that a butterfly spread requires the payment of four commissions to enter the trade. Brokerage firms' commission structures vary, but usually no additional fees are incurred if an option expires worthless. In the case of a short butterfly using put options, a price rally to above the highest strike at expiration is necessary for all the options to expire worthless and the entire original credit to be pocketed. Any lower price will generate additional commission costs to unwind the spread.

A short butterfly spread using calls traces out the same risk/reward profile as a butterfly spread using puts; both of the risk/reward diagrams assume zero commissions. In the case of a short butterfly spread using call options, a significant price down move in the underlying instrument (to below the lowest strike) is required to minimize commissions. Therefore, it pays the technician to formulate an educated guess as to the probable market direction. In this case study, this involves determining which of the converging trendlines is the strongest.

In Figure 12-1, quotes have already successfully tested the rising two-point trendline, although the test is still in progress. Since this trendline appears strongest, the probability of an upside move is judged to be higher. Therefore, to minimize commissions, the short butterfly spread using puts will be selected.

ORDER ENTRY

Option settlement (closing) prices have been utilized throughout this book to illustrate the possible trades. Since commissions play a potentially large role in this strategy, the bid-asked spread in the actual marketplace becomes important. Figure 12-2 illustrates an order ticket that has been used to ask for a butterfly spread quote only. After an indication of the market from the

Figure 12-2   Order Ticket Used to Obtain Bid and Asked Quote

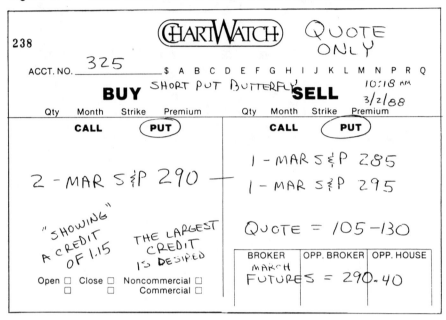

trading floor has been obtained, the actual short butterfly order with a specific credit can be entered. As noted on the order ticket in Figure 12-2, the quote from the options pit was 105-130. Entering the order at a credit of 120 would be a reasonable trading strategy and would have a good chance of being executed.

Short Put Butterfly

Short one March 285 put	=	2.30 credit
Long two March 290 puts	=	4.45 x 2 debit
Short one March 295 put	=	7.80 credit
		1.20 credit

Risk/Reward Parameters at Expiration

A tabular listing of profit or loss outcomes for each leg of the spread at various expiration prices is located in Table 12-1. Plotting the resulting values yields the specific risk/reward diagram in Figure 12-3. The discontinuities in the plot are clearly seen at the three strike prices.

Table 12-1   Tabular Risk/Reward of Short Butterfly at Expiration

Price at Expiration	280	285	290	295	300
Short 1 285 put	-5.00	0	0	0	0
Long 2 290 puts	+20.00	+10.00	0	0	0
Short 1 295 put	-15.00	-10.00	-5.00	0	0
Original credit	+1.20	+1.20	+1.20	+1.20	+1.20
Spread result	+1.20	+1.20	-3.80	+1.20	+1.20

Figure 12-3   Graphic Risk/Reward Profile of Short Butterfly Spread at Expiration

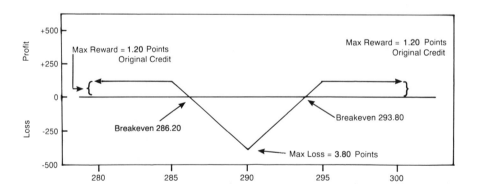

Figure 12-4   Outcome of the Converging Trendlines

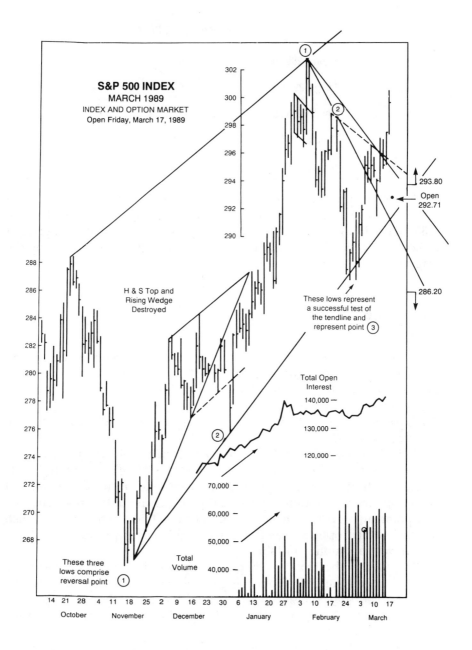

Table 12-2   Final Risk/Reward Accounting: Short Put Butterfly

	292.71 Settlement Price
Short 1 285 put	0
Long 2 290 puts	0
Short 1 295 put	-2.29
Original credit	+1.20
Result	-1.09

Breakeven prices (without commissions) are shown in Figure 12-3. The lower breakeven price of 286.20 is calculated by taking the lower strike price (285) and adding the original credit (1.20). The upper breakeven price of 293.80 is calculated by taking the upper strike (295) and subtracting the original credit (1.20).

OUTCOME

Figure 12-4 shows that the two-point up-sloping trendline became an infinitely more powerful three-point trendline. The ensuing price up move violated the shorter (in length) two-point down-sloping trendline. The significant price move forced by the converging trendlines moved the S&P 500 future far above the highest strike price put in the position as of the close Thursday, March 16.

But the actual settlement price of the S&P future on which the options are based was the special opening price on Friday. Here is where the "triple witching" effect of the multiple expirations of index futures, options, and equity options can disrupt the best-laid plans. Order imbalances caused a 6.99-point lower opening in the S&P 500 Index on Friday. The price on which the cash-settled options was based was 292.71! This produced the final risk/reward accounting in Table 12-2.

The effect of the triple witching anomaly was devastating to the results of the short put butterfly. From being in maximum profit territory by 5.90 points on Thursday's close, the gap open Friday turned the overall position into a 1.09 loser. No wonder the outside public is cautioned to avoid the quarterly expirations.

The technical analysis in this case study remains viable. Converging trendlines are expected to cause a significant price move. As always, timing in options trading is a two-edged sword!

CHAPTER 13

LONG-TERM CHARTS

LONG BUTTERFLY SPREAD

Options Strategy	When to Use	Technical Situation
Long Butterfly	Conservative trade using long-term options series	When measuring objective can be obtained from a weekly chart

The technical analysis covered in this book is heavily skewed toward discovering a directional price bias. Conventional options wisdom states that a long butterfly spread can be used by traders who are neutral (price-wise) on a particular instrument. This is true. But this options strategy will be used in this chapter when a significantly different (and in a particular direction) expiration price is very possible. The technical work will be concentrated on a long-term weekly chart.

June '87 Deutsche Mark Case Study

The long butterfly spread is a low-risk options strategy to take a shot at trading a more distant expiration options series in anticipation of a major price move. Although the probability of hitting the exact timing of a pattern achieving its objective may be small, the risk/reward ratios can be fantastic.

Long-term, weekly or monthly charts are used by traders to determine the direction of the major trend. Weekly futures charts seldom contain volume or open interest and are not practical for the active dealer/trader to use on a daily basis. Corporate hedgers often gain the best perspective from these charts. Classical formations do develop on weekly and month continuation charts.

Take the example of the possible H&S Top on the *daily* June 1987 D-Mark futures chart shown in Figure 13-1. This chart is interesting enough by itself, but look at what achieving the measuring objective of .5454 would do to the *weekly* chart in Figure 13-2.

Figure 13-1   Possible Small Head & Shoulders Top

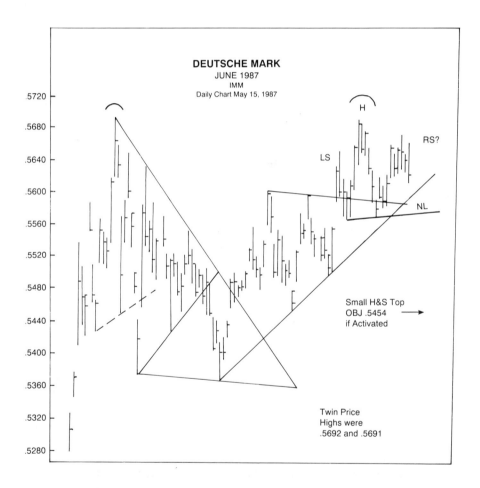

Figure 13-2 Possible Double Top—Weekly Continuation Chart

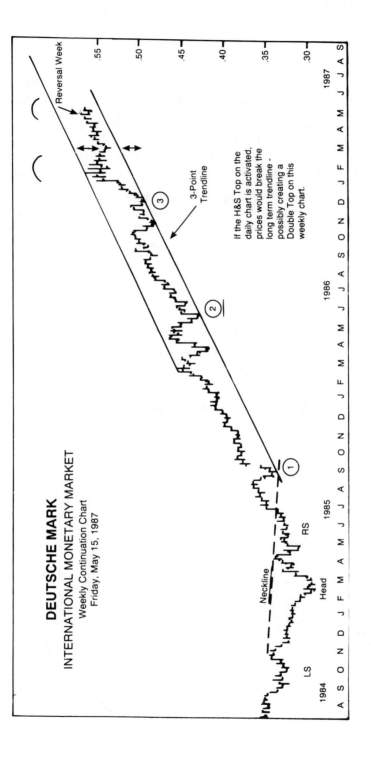

Given

1. The daily June D-Mark futures chart has a possible H&S Top. A close below the neckline at .5572 is needed to activate the formation.

2. Quickly achieving the minimum measuring objective of .5454 on the daily chart would penetrate an important 3-point up trendline on the weekly continuation chart. Note that this trendline began almost two years earlier in September 1985.

3. Breaking the weekly up trendline at the .5500 level would vastly increase the odds that the potential Double Top would be activated. This would take place on a Friday close below .5340 on the weekly chart, creating an objective of approximately .5000 for the nearest to expire future.

Statistics

1. Date: Friday, May 15, 1987.

2. September options expire September 4.

3. One tick on both the D-Mark futures and options = 12.50 $US.

4. Options prices for close May 15 were:

Table 13-1   Deutsche Mark Put Options, May 15, 1987

FRIDAY, MAY 15, 1987   DEUTSCHEMARK OPTIONS   BULLETIN #094

DEUTSCHEMARK PUT OPTIONS

STRIKE D-MARK PUT	OPEN RANGE (FUTURES SETT.	HIGH	LOW (FUTURES SETT.	CLOSING RANGE .00 UNCH)	SETT. PRICE & PT. CHGE.	##/ FACTOR	CISES	VOLUME TRADES CLEARED	OPEN INTEREST	--CONTRACT-- HIGH	LOW
MAY87 D-MARK PUT	(FUTURES SETT.			.00 UNCH)							
TOTAL											
JNE87 D-MARK PUT	(FUTURES SETT.			.5657 + 43)							
46	----	----	----	CAB	CAB --	---- ----	----		629 UNCH	.48	.01
47	----	----	----	CAB	CAB --	---- ----	----		698 UNCH	1.33	.01
48	----	----	----	CAB	CAB --	---- ----	----		949 UNCH	1.52B	.01
49	----	----	----	CAB	CAB --	---- ----	----		1226 UNCH	2.10	.01
50	----	----	----	CAB	CAB --	---- ----	----		2370 UNCH	2.57B	.01
51	----	----	----	CAB	CAB --	.000 ----	----		2056 - 2	3.28	.01
52	.01	.01	.01	.01	.01 UNCH	.000 ----	----	117	2490 - 54	3.96B	.01
53	.02	.03	.02	.02	.02 UNCH	.007 ----	----	3717	6989 + 2797	1.98	.02
54	.05	.07	*.05	.05	.05 - 2	.040 ----	----	623	6098 - 15	2.13	.05
55	.14	.14	*.09	.10	.10 - 7	.143 ----	----	634	8413 - 119	2.32	.09
56	.40	.44	*.30	.30	.31 - 17	.347 ----	----	1168	6333 + 118	2.76	.30
57	.92	.94B	*.82	.82	.80 - 29	.606 ----	----	12	1097 + 7	3.30B	.82
58	----	----	1.70A	1.75A	1.55 - 39	.820 ----	----	----	117 UNCH	4.18B	1.53
59	----	----	2.65A	2.66A	2.47 - 41	.940 ----	----	----	18 UNCH	4.77B	2.50A
60	----	----	----	3.86N	3.43 - 43	.985 ----	----	----	1 UNCH	4.85B	3.40A
TOTAL								6271	39484 + 2732		
JLY87 D-MARK PUT	(FUTURES SETT.			.00 UNCH)							
52	----	----	----	.05N	.04 - 1	.009 ----	----	----	154 UNCH	.07	.05
53	----	----	----	.08N	.06 - 2	.031 ----	----	----	326 UNCH	.41	.10
54	.10	.11	*.10	.10	.09 - 5	.080 ----	----	336	828 + 34	.49	.10
55	.25	.28	*.24A	.28	.21 - 7	.171 ----	----	4	424 + 2	.60B	.24A
56	.50	.50	*.47	.48	.42 - 14	.306 ----	----	18	529 + 7	1.05	.47
57	1.05	1.05	*.92A	.92A	.81 - 22	.472 ----	----	10	307 + 10	1.40	.92A
TOTAL								368	2568 + 313		
AUG87 D-MARK PUT	(FUTURES SETT.			.00 UNCH)							
54	.22	.28	*.22	.28	.24 - 7	.141 ----	----	15	111 + 11	.43	.22
55	.43	.43	*.43	.43	.43 NEW	.232 ----	----	10	10 + 6	.43	.43
56	----	----	*.78A	.78A	.72 - 12	.347 ----	----	----	101 UNCH	1.10	.78A
TOTAL								25	222 + 21		
SEP87 D-MARK PUT	(FUTURES SETT.			.5711 + 45)							
48	----	----	----	.04N	02 - 1	.002 ----	----	----	841 UNCH	1.10	.05
49	----	----	----	.04N	.04 UNCH	.006 ----	----	----	510 UNCH	1.50B	.05A
50	----	----	----	.07N	.07 UNCH	.014 ----	----	----	711 UNCH	1.95B	.07
51	----	----	----	.11N	.10 - 1	.031 ----	----	----	908 UNCH	2.50	.12A
52	.15	.15	*.15	.15	.14 - 3	.061 ----	----	3	920 + 5	3.05B	.15
53	.22	.22	*.22	.24A@.22	.22 - 6	.107 ----	----	25	1992 + 25	1.80	.22
54	----	----	*.40A	.40A	.37 - 8	.174 ----	----	11	1633 + 11	2.00	.40A
55	.58	.68	*.58	.60	.59 - 11	.261 ----	----	59	3509 + 6	2.50	.58
56	----	----	*.93A	.98A	.91 - 14	.363 ----	----	3	2848 + 3	2.85	.93A
57	1.54	1.54	*1.45A	1.45A	1.34 - 20	.475 ----	----	22	1227 + 22	3.55B	1.42
58	----	----	*2.03A	2.03A	1.90 - 25	.586 ----	----	----	1 UNCH	2.40B	2.03A
59	----	----	----	2.87N	2.57 - 30	.689 ----	----	----	2 UNCH	3.17B	2.60
60	----	----	----	3.65N	3.32 - 33	.778 ----	----	----	2 UNCH	4.08B	3.38
TOTAL								123	16094 + 70		
DEC87 D-MARK PUT	(FUTURES SETT.			.5769 + 47)							
50	.19	.19	*.16A	.18A	.16 - 3	.039 ----	----	9	463 + 9	.23	.16A
51	.27	.27	*.27	.27	.24 - 6	.064 ----	----	9	51 + 9	.35	.27
52	----	----	*.32A	.32A	.31 - 5	.098 ----	----	----	1397 UNCH	.75	.32A
53	.42	.48B	*.42	.42	.46 - 7	.144 ----	----	500	575 + 400	.96B	.42
54	.68@.70	.70	*.68	.70	.66 - 7	.201 ----	----	20	538 + 20	1.80	.68
55	.90	.94B	*.90	.90	.90 - 9	.269 ----	----	171	665 + 1	2.19B	.90
56	1.24	1.24	*1.24	1.24	1.21 - 15	.345 ----	----	350	1154 + 200	2.27	1.24
57	1.75	1.75	*1.67A	1.70	1.60 - 20	.426 ----	----	160	438 + 115	2.45B	1.67A
58	2.18	2.18	*2.18	2.18	2.10 - 23	.509 ----	----	100	103 + 100	2.45	2.18
TOTAL								1319	5384 + 854		

Trading Plan

The September options expiration series has more than 3 1/2 months remaining to expiration. This should be enough time for the possible topping process on the D-Mark chart to be well underway. Since the .5000 level is the potential objective, the 50 strike will be selected for the "body" of the spread.

A long butterfly can be constructed using either calls or puts, and the resulting risk/reward diagram without commissions will be similar. But the extremely large directional bias toward the bearish side of the market dictates the selection of low-cost puts in this case study. The "wings" of the spread will be the long positions in the option strikes on either side of the 50 strike "body."

LONG D-MARK BUTTERFLY

Long 1 Sept 49 put   =   .04 debit

Short 2 Sept 50 puts   =   .07 x 2 = .14 credit

Long 1 Sept 51 put   =   <u>.11 debit</u>

                     .01 debit = maximum risk

Delta of spread = -.006 + 2(.014) - .031 = -.009

Table 13-2 contains a tabular risk/reward statement of the selected strategy. A plot of the payoff amounts at expiration is shown in Figure 13-3. Any expiration price above the zero line within the "profit pyramid" represents a successful trade. A quick look at Figure 13-3 shows the fantastic risk to reward ratio: 1 to 99! The long butterfly spread selected and the various prices stated were simply taken from the CME closing range quote sheet in Table 13-1, so this position is hypothetical. In actual practice, it would be difficult, if not impossible, to find a local pit trader to take the other side of this trade for only a one-tick (12.50$) profit potential. This strongly suggests the strategy of legging into the position.

In theory, the maximum profit potential would be realized if the D-Mark future is exactly at the middle 50 strike at expiration on September 4. This would result in a 99-tick gross profit per spread (1,237.50$). The risk is the net debit plus commissions.

Table 13-2   Tabular Risk/Reward of Long Butterfly at Expiration

Price at Expiration	48	49	50	51	52	54
Long 1 49 put	+1.00	0	0	0	0	0
Short 2 50 puts	-4.00	-2.00	0	0	0	0
Long 1 51 put	+3.00	+2.00	+1.00	0	0	0
.01 Initial debit (cost of spread)	-.01	-.01	-.01	-.01	-.01	-.01
Spread result	-.01	-.01	+.99	-.01	-.01	-.01

Figure 13-3   Graphic Risk/Reward Profile of Long Butterfly Spread at Expiration

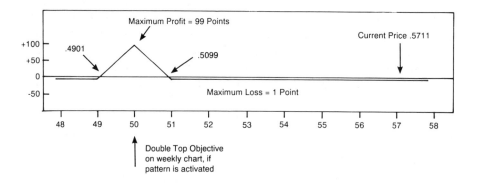

Commission Considerations

At any expiration price, the initial four commissions paid to execute the long butterfly spread are a factor. As quotes move below .5099 going into expiration, the 51 strike puts move into the money. Additional transaction costs become necessary. It is this leg of the spread that is the money maker. At an expiration price below .4900, all the puts would be in-the-money. Obviously, commissions represent a significant loss in percentage terms. This is why this strategy of creating out-of-the-money long butterfly spreads is most often considered only by floor traders or market makers.

D-MARK BUTTERFLY SPREAD OUTCOME

The weekly chart in Figure 13-4 says it all:

1.   The two-year up trendline was penetrated.

2.   The Double Top was activated.

3.   A significant rally into September caused the Sept 49-50-51 D-Mark long put butterfly spread to expire worthless.

Figure 13-4   Possible H&S Top on a Weekly Chart

TRY IT AGAIN?

The weekly D-Mark chart in Figure 13-4 now looks like a very large Head & Shoulders Top is developing. This outlook is enhanced by the daily chart in Figure 13-5 with the small H&S Top. An eventual downside objective of as low as .4850 can be obtained if the weekly H&S Top is activated. Theoretical placement of another long put butterfly spread will be investigated. The 50 strike price D-Mark put expiring in early December will be used as the body of the long butterfly.

Put option prices for the December D-Mark expiration (and beyond) are located in Table 13-3. Note that the Dec 49 put has a price listed as CAB, for cabinet. A price less than the minimum price fluctuation is often available for traders on both sides of a closing trade in an out-of-the-money option. It is referred to as a *cabinet trade*.

In this case study, a new opening position is being created in the Dec 49 put. Thus, a price of .01, or one tick, is used in the illustration of the 49-50-51 long butterfly spread.

Figure 13-5   Head & Shoulders Top

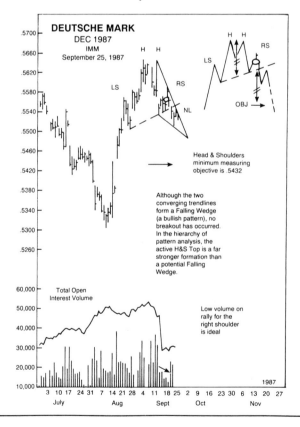

Table 13-3   Deutsche Mark Put Options, September 25, 1987

STRIKE	OPEN RANGE	HIGH	LOW	CLOSING RANGE	SETT. & PT.	PRICE CHGE.	IOM RISK ## FACTOR	EXER-CISES	VOLUME TRADES CLEARED	OPEN INTEREST		--CONTRACT-- HIGH	LOW
SEP87	D-MARK	PUT	(FUTURES SETT.)	.0000 UNCH)									
TOTAL				.00 UNCH)									
OCT87	D-MARK	PUT	(FUTURES SETT.)	.00 UNCH)									
52	----	----	----	CAB	CAB	----	.000	----	----	2114	UNCH	.41B	.01
53	.03	.03	.02A	.02A	.01	-1	.011	----	2	1594	UNCH	.71B	.02
54	.07	.07	.07	.07	.07	+1	.099	----	203	2243	+203	1.29	.04
55	.25	.26	.23	.25	.24	+2	.376	----	470	3358	+59	1.60B	.15A
56	.83	.84B	.80A	.83	.83	+5	.737	----	1	994	-5	.95B	.50
TOTAL									676	10303	+257		
NOV87	D-MARK	PUT	(FUTURES SETT.)	.00 UNCH)									
53	----	.09B	----	.09B	.09	+1	.092	----	----	562	UNCH	.93	.07
54	----	.22B	----	.21N	.23	+2	.225	----	----	631	UNCH	.61	.16
55	.55	.55	.51	.51	.53	+3	.423	----	365	693	+241	.65B	.38
56	----	1.05B	----	1.05B	1.08	+6	.639	----	----	204	UNCH	1.14B	.80A
TOTAL									365	2909	+241		
DEC87	D-MARK	PUT	(FUTURES SETT.)	.5532 -8)									
49	----	----	----	CAB	CAB	----	.001	----	----	110	UNCH	.02	.01
50	----	----	----	.03N	.03	UNCH	.007	----	----	1615	UNCH	.31	.02
51	----	----	----	.05N	.05	UNCH	.026	----	----	1275	UNCH	.47	.04
52	----	----	----	.08N	.08	UNCH	.069	----	----	4172	-52	.77	.07
53	.22	.22	.19	.20B	.21	+1	.150	----	801	4031	-873	1.16	.16
54	.42	.43	.38	.41	.41	+2	.277	----	208	5151	-95	1.80	.31
55	.77	.77	.72	.74	.75	+4	.437	----	396	6096	+41	2.30	.58
56	1.25	1.27B	1.25	1.25	1.29	+5	.605	----	2	3384	-2	3.01	.92
57	----	1.98B	----	1.98B	1.99	+4	.753	----	----	2527	UNCH	3.84	1.53A
58	2.83	2.83	2.83	2.83	2.83	+7	.863	----	3	439	+3	4.87	2.07A
59	----	----	----	3.66N	3.71	+5	.933	----	----	11	-978	3.80	3.10A
TOTAL									1410	28811			
MAR88	D-MARK	PUT	(FUTURES SETT.)	.5576 -10)									
50	----	----	----	.12N	.12	UNCH	.041	----	----	1005	UNCH	.44	10A
51	----	----	----	.19N	.19	UNCH	.077	----	----	46	UNCH	.40	.20A
52	----	----	----	.29N	.30	+1	.131	----	----	828	UNCH	1.00B	.13A
53	----	----	----	.47N	.48	+2	.205	----	----	1629	UNCH	1.40	.40
54	.73	.73	.73	.73	.73	+2	.297	----	1	2034	UNCH	1.88B	.63A
55	----	1.08B	----	1.08B	1.09	+3	.402	----	----	2982	UNCH	2.35	.90
56	1.53	1.53	1.53	1.53	1.55	+5	.513	----	4	2144	+2	3.03B	1.30A
57	2.12	2.12	2.12	2.12	2.14	+6	.621	----	3	405	UNCH	3.24B	1.74
58	----	----	----	2.75N	2.82	+7	.719	----	----	8	UNCH	2.95	2.36A
TOTAL									8	11081	+2		
JNE88	D-MARK	PUT	(FUTURES SETT.)	.5628 -7)									
53	----	----	----	.69N	.71	+2	.215	----	----	650	UNCH	.72B	.53
55	1.32	#1.32	1.32	1.32	1.32	+4	.371	----	1	3	+1	1.32	1.22
56	----	#1.73B	----	1.73B	1.74	+4	.459	----	----	220	UNCH	1.73B	1.47
57	----	----	----	2.20N	2.25	+5	.547	----	----	428	UNCH	2.20B	1.90
58	----	----	----	2.80N	2.86	+6	.631	----	----	80	UNCH	2.74B	2.25A
TOTAL									1	1381	+1		

	VOLUME	OPEN INTEREST		----YEARS AGO---- VOLUME	OPN INT.
TOTAL DEUTSCHEMARK CALLS	3106	62330	- 2296	2727	39848
TOTAL DEUTSCHEMARK PUTS	2460	53666	- 477	2801	36143
TOTAL DEUTSCHEMARK OPTIONS	5566	115996	- 2773	5528	75991

CAB (CABINET TRANSACTION) -- DM = 0.0008
++Approximate Delta, used in computation of Option Margins for Members

SECOND LONG BUTTERFLY ATTEMPT

Long Dec 49-50-51 put butterfly
Cost = -.01 + 2(.03) - .05 = 0$ = maximum risk
Delta of spread = -.001 + 2(.007) - .026 = -.013

Simply using the quotes from Table 13-3 yields a spread with zero risk. Obviously, this cannot be executed as a spread. It means that a trader with this technical view will have to leg into the spread. Legging into a long butterfly with the hope of ultimately locking in a zero-risk position does possess intriguing qualities.

OUTCOME

Figure 13-6 shows that the possible H&S Top on the weekly chart never formed. There is still no bottom in the U.S. Dollar! The second attempt at a long butterfly put spread resulted in a spread that would have expired worthless.

Technically, this was *not* a Head & Shoulders failure. It *was* a failure of the pattern to form. This is another example of using an options strategy to lead off that produced a loss that was much less than an outright short position.

Figure 13-6   H&S Top Never Formed

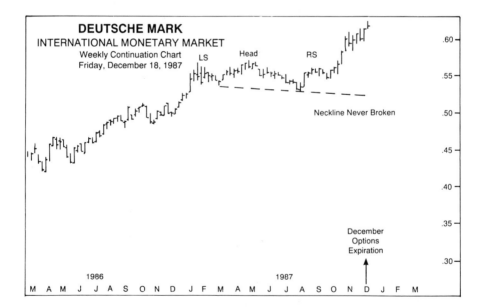

SUMMARY

Neither of the two theoretical attempts to profit from a long butterfly spread resulted in a profit. This does not mean that the strategy is worthless. Some trading styles lean toward buying far out-of-the-money options. If some price progress in the favorable direction does occur, it may be possible to leg into a long butterfly. The trader might then own an options position "for free." Planning ahead, leaving room to short options for the body of the long butterfly, is an approach worth considering.

CHAPTER 14

KEY REVERSAL DAY

WRITING A VERTICAL SPREAD FOR A CREDIT

Options Strategy	When to Use	Technical Situation
Vertical Credit Spread	Directional bias close to expiration	Minor trend change indicator

The prior chapters have emphasized the use of debit spreads because of their specific (limited) risk parameter and suitability for follow-up action. But a popular strategy with professional traders is to write vertical spreads for a credit, placing time decay in their favor. This is especially true in an options series that is close (within three weeks) to expiration.

The case study in this chapter will examine a Key Reversal Day on the S&P 500 futures chart. The location of this minor trend change indicator was such that a price high for an outer right shoulder of a developing Complex Head & Shoulders Top could be developing. Options on the S&P 500 futures were expiring on the opening 18 calendar days later.

June '91 S&P 500 Case Study

Figure 14-1 shows that a Key Reversal Day high posting was made on the June 1991 S&P 500 futures chart on Monday, June 3, 1991. A Key Reversal posting is composed of a higher high together with a lower "close" on a bar chart. Especially intriguing is the technical possibility that the price high could mark the top of an outer right shoulder in a developing Complex Head & Shoulders Top.

181

Figure 14-1   Key Reversal Day for High of an Outer Right Shoulder of a Possible H&S Top

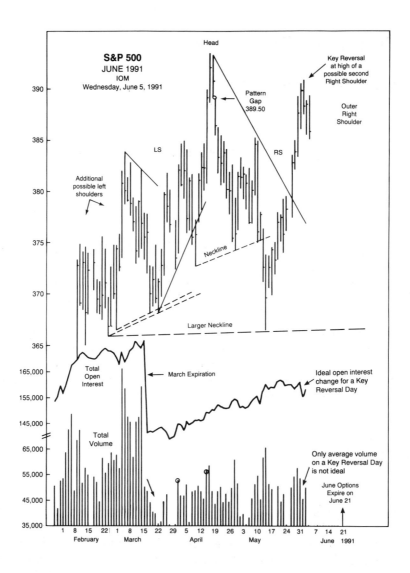

The Key Reversal (K-R) Day worked on the next trading session by virtue of the lower daily low than the K-R Day. But the higher close (by .25) would have made longer-term traders wary of placing outright short futures positions. The next trading session, Wednesday, June 5, saw a price rally attempt early. The selloff going into the close strongly suggested that the K-R high was holding a lid on the price rally. At this time, writing a vertical call spread for a credit became a strategy worth investigating.

The June S&P 500 future settled at 385.90 on Wednesday, June 5 (Figure 14-1). A long 395 versus short 390 June call spread would profit from an unchanged to lower market by the option expiration on the open 16 calendar

Table 14-1   Typical Brokerage House Statement

DATE 06/05/91

DATE	QUANTITY BOUGHT	SOLD	COMMODITY/ DESCRIPTION	TRADE PRICE	AMOUNT DEBIT	CREDIT
			++++++++++++++++++++++++++++++++ OPTION TRADE TRANSACTIONS ++++++++++++++++++++++++++++++++++			
6/05/91		1 1*	JUN 91 CALL 390 S&P 500 EXPIRATION DATE 06/20/1991	.280		1,400.00
			OPTION NET PREMIUM PAID/RECEIVED			1,400.00
			OPTION TRADE COMMISSIONS		12.50	
			OPTION EXCHANGE FEE		.35	
			OPTION NFA FEE		.12	
6/05/91	1 1*		JUN 91 CALL 395 S&P 500 EXPIRATION DATE 06/20/1991	.170	850.00	
			OPTION NET PREMIUM PAID/RECEIVED		850.00	
			OPTION TRADE COMMISSIONS		12.50	
			OPTION EXCHANGE FEE		.35	
			OPTION NFA FEE		.12	
			NET CREDIT.			524.06 $US

days later. The maximum profit possible would be the net credit received. A maximum loss parameter also exists. This is the difference between the legs of the options spread minus the credit. An actual brokerage house statement in Table 14-1 shows a spread trade made during the trading session.

The gross credit received was 1400 - 850 = 550$. Subtracting two commissions of 12.50$, option exchange fees of 0.70$ and National Futures Association (NFA) fees of 0.24$, a net credit of 524.06$ results.

Option settlement prices for Wednesday, June 5 are listed below. Given these values, the open trade statement for the vertical bear L390/S395 call spread is shown in Table 14-2.

FUTURES OPTIONS

S&P 500 STOCK INDEX (CME) $500 times premium

Strike	Calls—Settle			Puts—Settle		
Price	Jun-c	Jly-c	Au-c	Jun-p	Jly-p	Aug-p
375	12.25	17.15	....	1.40	3.65	5.80
380	8.40	13.50	15.80	2.50	4.95	7.25
385	5.20	10.25	....	4.30	6.65	9.05
390	2.85	7.50	9.80	6.95	8.85	....
.395	1.40	5.25	....	10.45	11.50	....
400	0.65	3.50	5.35	14.70	14.70	....

Est. vol. 6,116; Tues vol. 1,370 calls; 4,041 puts
Open Interest Tues; 28,745 calls; 56,781 puts

Table 14-2   Open Trade Statement

DATE 6/05/91

	QUANTITY		COMMODITY/		TRADE	AMOUNT	
DATE	BOUGHT	SOLD	DESCRIPTION		PRICE	DEBIT	CREDIT

++ OPEN POSITIONS ++

LEGEND: FSP= FUTURES SETTLEMENT PRICE   MV= MARKET VALUE
        AP= AVERAGE PRICE   ITM= IN THE MONEY PER/CONTRACT
        SP= OPTIONS SETTLEMENT PRICE

6/05/91		1	JUN 91 CALL 390 S&P 500		.280	25.00	
		1*	EXPIRATION DATE 06/20/91				
			FSP= 385.90 SP=	.285			
			MV= 1,425.00 ITM=	0.00 PER/CONTRACT			
6/05/91	1		JUN 91 CALL 395 S&P 500		.170	150.00	
	1*		EXPIRATION DATE 06/20/91				
			FSP= 385.90 SP=	.140			
			MV= 700.00 ITM=	0.00 PER/CONTRACT			

OUTCOME

Figure 14-2 shows that the S&P quotes did indeed remain below the lower strike of the S390/L395 call spread at the expiration. The brokerage statement in Table 14-3 shows the outcome. Both options were, in effect,

Figure 14-2   June Option Expiration

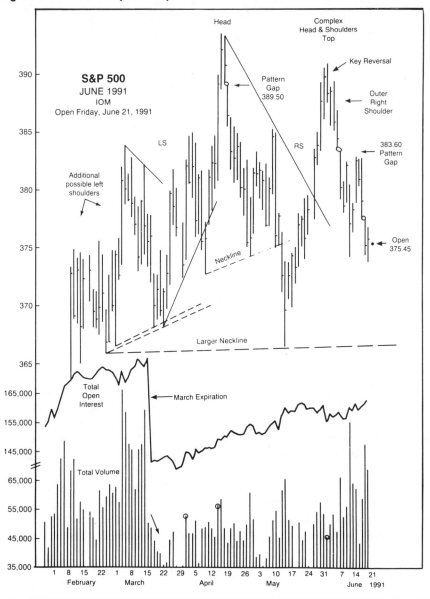

Table 14-3   Statement Showing Vertical Spread at Expiration

DATE **06/21/91**

DATE	QUANTITY BOUGHT	QUANTITY SOLD	COMMODITY/ DESCRIPTION	TRADE PRICE	AMOUNT DEBIT	AMOUNT CREDIT
			###			
			++++++++++++++++++ OPEN POSITIONS +++++++++++++++++++++++++++++++++++++++			
	LEGEND:	FSP= FUTURES SETTLEMENT PRICE	MV= MARKET VALUE			
		AP= AVERAGE PRICE	ITM= IN THE MONEY PER/CONTRACT			
		SP= OPTIONS SETTLEMENT PRICE				
6/05/91		1 1*	JUN 91 CALL 390 S&P 500 EXPIRATION DATE 06/20/91 FSP= 375.45 SP= 9999999 MV= 12.50 ITM= 0.00 PER/CONTRACT	.280		1,387.50
6/05/91	1 1*		JUN 91 CALL 395 S&P 500 EXPIRATION DATE 06/20/91 FSP= 375.45 SP= 9999999 MV= 12.50 ITM= 0.00 PER/CONTRACT	.170	837.50	
			NET CREDIT			524.06 $US

---

worthless. The clearinghouse computer shows an options settlement price of 9999999 to indicate a "cabinet" or minimum value of 12.50$ on June 21. The gross profit was the 550$ difference between the credit and debit shown.

MINOR TREND CHANGE INDICATORS

There are four popular price configurations that are categorized as minor trend change indicators. These are the: Key Reversal Day, Inside Range Day, Outside Range Day and Mid-Range Close. They all indicate that the forces of the bulls and bears have reached at least a temporary equilibrium. The forces previously in control of the market are losing momentum, but the opposing forces have not gathered enough strength to turn the trend. The tide is expected to turn soon - usually the next trading session.

The four minor trend change indicators are predominately used by short term traders/dealers looking for what might happen next. But longer term traders can also benefit by looking for one of these indicators at reversal point 4 in a continuation pattern (Triangle or Wedge) or reversal point 5 in an H&S or Broadening Formation. The assumption is made that the short term price gyrations are coming to an end and a more significant price move is about to begin.

Writing options that are soon to expire can be an excellent trading approach after a minor trend change indicator is posted on a daily chart. Creating a vertical spread for a credit establishes a limited risk parameter to the trade. A continued sideways price move or one in the expected direction should yield a worthwhile result.

CHAPTER 15

VOLATILITY FORECASTING

A major contingent of options traders concentrates very heavily on the volatility component of pricing. These volatility traders try to isolate this variable and trade it. Usually this involves constructing a delta-neutral strategy (the difficult part is *keeping* the strategy price neutral) and taking advantage of seemingly under- or overpriced options. If the traders' view on volatility proves correct, the realized volatility that occurs will generate a profitable trade. Even the directional trader must be aware of the added profit or loss that will result from a change in implied volatility. This chapter will explore some technical aspects of volatility charts.

STRATEGIC IMPORTANCE OF VOLATILITY

Figure C-2 in Appendix C illustrates the theoretical shape of an options price using a typical options pricing model. Note that the time premium of an at-the-money option is the greatest. Since changes in implied volatility directly affect the premium of an at-the-money option to the greatest extent, this option becomes the price vehicle for speculating in over- or understated implied volatility.

Historical volatility of any market over long periods tends to revert toward a long-term average. This is referred to as the *mean reverting tendency*. An options trader trying to determine whether to buy or sell volatility would undertake, at minimum, a four-step process:

1. Is the current reading of historical volatility of the underlying above or below its long-term average?

2. Is the short-term historical volatility (perhaps 20 days) currently increasing or decreasing?

3. Is the implied volatility in the option itself above or below the historical volatility? Is implied volatility currently increasing or decreasing?

4. Is the underlying product subject to distinct seasonal influences? If so, the seasonal trend in volatility, both historical and implied, must be included in the analysis. This is more prevalent in the agricultural markets than in the financial instruments.

Figure 15-1   Volatility Overview

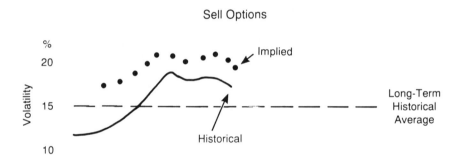

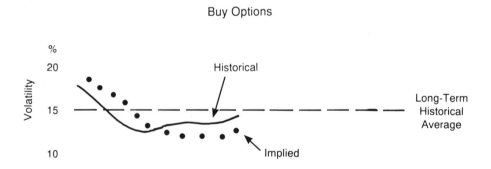

The volatility overview in Figure 15-1 illustrates the two most clear-cut extremes in which a trader should incorporate a volatility view into any options strategy.

Sell Options

1. Historical volatility above long-term average
2. Near-term historical volatility declining
3. Implied volatility above historical volatility and declining

Buy Options

1. Historical volatility below long-term average
2. Near-term historical volatility rising
3. Implied volatility below historical volatility and rising

IDIOSYNCRASIES

Implied volatility does exhibit idiosyncrasies. It tends, for instance, to make spike tops versus rounding bottoms in the physical commodity and metals options. In the stock index markets, implied volatility often increases as prices move lower and traders become concerned about a 1987-style crash. These idiosyncrasies are due to the psychological human nature involved in the determination of the actual options price.

As options trading on an instrument becomes more mature, the variations in implied volatility may experience a damping effect. For example, the implied volatility on D-Mark futures options on the IMM experienced very limited movement on either side of 12 1/2 percent through all of 1991. This was in contrast to wide price swings that generated considerable swings in historic volatility readings between 8 and 20 percent during 1991.

TECHNICAL ANALYSIS AND THE USE OF VEGA

A theoretical options pricing model produces a statistic referred to by traders as vega. Vega is the sensitivity of an option's theoretical value to changes in implied volatility. * Vega measures the amount of option premium gained (lost) when implied volatility increases (decreases) one percentage point. Vega is most often quoted in price points (or ticks). For example, an option with a vega of .04 would gain four ticks in fair value if implied volatility increased 1 percent.

A trader with a volatility forecast different from what the market is currently expecting can profit if the forecast is correct. If the current implied volatility is lower than what the trader believes will be true, the bias is to purchase (undervalued) options and execute a delta-neutral hedge. To remain delta neutral, the overall position must be constantly examined and readjusted. For this reason, volatility spreads are more often the bailiwick of floor traders with substantially lower transaction costs.

But speculators who are not exchange members must also be aware of what a change in volatility would do to their positions. Vega is the option model derivative that allows this risk to be quantified. The following examples show some of the extreme variability that existed on the implied volatility graphs of the financial instrument futures options in the late 1980s. A technician will be quick to observe the possibility of classical bar charting price patterns—especially topping formations. Since implied volatility is a function of traders' emotions, there is no reason why its chart should not be treated in a classic technical fashion.

Figure 15-2 is an implied volatility chart of the IMM Japanese Yen futures put options. It represents only the closest-to-the-money options. An implied volatility chart can be constructed using any single option or combination. One convention (as used here) is to plot the mean of the closest-to-the-money, first-in-the-money and first-out-of-the-money implied volatilities. Technicians will see the possibility of a Double Top in Figure 15-2. A posting below 10 1/2 percent would imply a down move in implied volatility to 7 1/2 percent. This is not an unreasonable forecast. Implied volatility had been as low as 7 percent in the previous month.

Armed with the vega statistic of .06, a trader could calculate the theoretical decline in fair value if the implied volatility dropped from the current level of 11 percent to the possible 7 1/2 percent target: 6 X 3 1/2 = 19 ticks. As usual when entering the theoretical world, the phrase "all other paramaeters remain unchanged" must be added!

---

*Mathematicians would refer to this sensitivity as a partial derivative of the option's theoretical value with respect to volatility. They would also prefer to denote it with a true Greek letter such as kappa or zeta, but for options traders the v in vega is easier to link with the v in volatility.

Figure 15-2   Implied Volatility: IMM Japanese Yen Puts

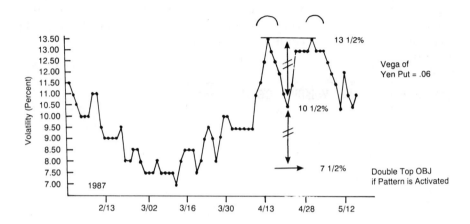

Figure 15-3 shows an implied volatility chart for IMM D-Mark put options. Implied volatility looks relatively low. The vega of these at-the-money puts is .04. This means that for every 1 percent increase in implied volatility, the at-the-money put option would be expected to increase 4 ticks in price.

Figure 15-3   Implied Volatility: IMM D-Mark Puts

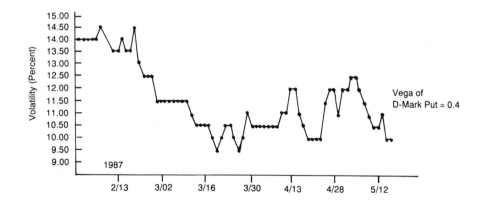

The U.S. Treasury bond futures implied volatility chart in Figure 15-4 presents the opportunity to play "what-if" games with an options pricing model. In this instance, a hand-held programmable calculator was used. Technically, a Complex H&S Top could be forming on the implied volatility chart. A Double Top would be present for the head. A decline to below 14 percent would forecast a continued decline to 9.6 percent to a classical bar chartist.

Figure 15-4   Implied Volatility: CBOT T-Bond Puts

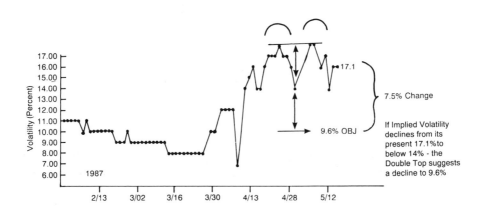

SOLVING FOR IMPLIED VOLATILITY

To solve an options pricing model for implied volatility of an option on a futures contract, a trader must input the six necessary variables. This requires inputting the actual value of the traded option. On May 19, 1987, the premium of the 88-00 T-bond put option was 3-26.

Input:

1. Strike: 88-00

2. Put or Call: P

3. Premium: 3-26 (actual value 5/19/87)

4. Futures price: 87-06

5. Days to maturity: 95

6. Short-term rate: 7%

Output:

1. Implied volatility = 17.1%

2. Delta = -0.52

3. Vega = 0.11

The vega of 0.11 for the at-the-money option (note the delta of -0.52) was the desired variable. This implies that an instantaneous change in implied volatility of 17.1 - 9.6 = 7.5 would produce a reduction in theoretical fair value of 7.5 X 11 or 82.5 ticks. One tick on the T-bond options is 1/64th.

As a check, a trader can run the fair value model in the traditional fashion. The inputs will now include a volatility figure (9.6 percent), and the algorithm will solve for the fair value:

Output: Fair value = 2-07

The actual options price was 3-26. A new fair value of 2-07 means the options must have declined in price by (3-26 - 2-07) = 83/64ths. This is close to the same as the solution using vega and multiplying it by the expected change in implied volatility.

The assumption of an instantaneous change in implied volatility of 7 1/2 percent is probably unrealistic. Therefore, assume that one week passes before the lower volatility objective is reached. The model is run using the targeted 9.6 implied volatility figure and only 88 days to expiration. The fair value is now 2-03. The additional passage of time took 4/64ths off the theoretical price.

This particular model (a hand-held version) did not produce the options derivative theta. Theta is the amount of premium lost as one day passes. If this statistic was available, the theoretical loss in options premium could have been calculated. Theta is not a linear function, so it is useful only for a short time frame.

CHAPTER 16

ELLIOTT WAVE COUNT

STRATEGIES FOR FLAT MARKETS

Options Strategy	When to Use	Technical Situation
Short Straddle	Expect stagnating price activity	1. Volume and open interest declining
Short Strangle	Market going sideways and stagnating	2. Triangle forming on weekly chart 3. In Elliott Wave II or IV
Neutral Calendar Spread	Expect stagnating price activity	4. In-between support and resistance

It is easy to state that an options trader should write options when implied volatility is high and the market is expected to vacillate net sideways. The technical problem is finding this situation. The Elliott Wave Principle offers a possible solution.

Waves I, III and V are deemed to be *impulse waves* that occur in the direction of the major price trend. Waves II and IV are *corrective waves*. In corrective waves, prices are expected to move net sideways or against the direction of the major trend. Corrective waves are composed of three waves labeled A-B-C.

Often the A-B-C corrections take the form of a classical bar charting price pattern—the Triangle or Wedge patterns in particular. It is during these corrections that an options strategy designed for a relatively flat market comes into play.

OVERVIEW OF OPTIONS STRATEGIES FOR FLAT MARKETS

Three options strategies that might be employed when a market correction is probable are the short straddle, short strangle or calendar spread. Figure 16-1 is a schematic diagram of an idealized Elliott Wave count. Corrective waves II and IV consist of a Triangle and Wedge pattern.

Figure 16-1   Elliott Wave/Options Strategies

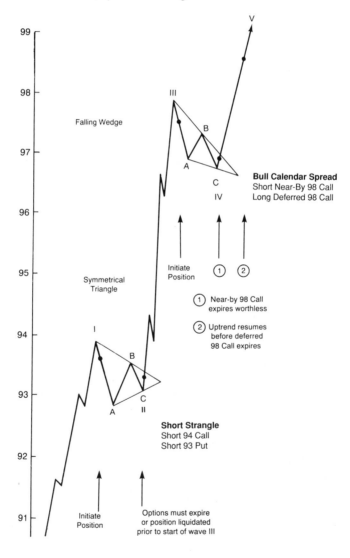

A calendar spread will be investigated in depth in this chapter. It will be placed based on two technical disciplines: (1) an Elliott Wave count and (2) a possible small near-term classical bearish price pattern, but long-term a very large bullish pattern.

SHORT STRADDLE

A short straddle consists of a short call and short put of the same expiration and is typically initiated using the at-the-money strike. As seen in Figure 16-2, the risk is unlimited, and the maximum reward is equal to the premiums received if the underlying instrument was exactly at the strike price at expiration.

SHORT STRANGLE

The short strangle is also referred to as a combination write. Both an out-of-the-money call and put are sold with the same expiration date but different strikes. A generic risk/reward profile is shown in Figure 16-2. Note the unlimited risk in either direction. The maximum reward is the options premium received.

Figure 16-2   Risk/Reward Profiles: Short Straddle and Short Strangle

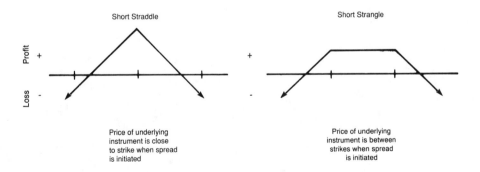

A trader expecting a Wave II or Wave IV correction would initiate a short straddle or short strangle strategy. The options must expire (ideally worthless) before the start of the next impulse wave. If a clear-cut breakout on the price chart occurs, the strategy must be liquidated.

CALENDAR SPREAD

A calendar spread, also referred to as a time spread, takes advantage of the accelerated time decay of a near-to-expire option. An option with a shorter expiration date is sold while a longer-term option is purchased. If the exercise price is the same, a debit spread is created and it is referred to as a long calendar spread. There is a maximum risk parameter in this spread equal to the net debit. This can be seen in the risk/reward profile in Figure 16-3. The trader would ideally like to see the near-term option expire worthless. If the major trend then resumes, the longer-dated option could prove to be very lucrative. Obviously, timing is paramount in this strategy.

An intriguing possibility in a calendar spread is diagonalizing the position. This involves purchase of a longer-dated option with a different strike than the nearby option sold short. If the option purchased is far enough out-of-the-money, the diagonal spread can be placed at a credit. This means that a correct forecast of near-term price movement could result in owning an option "for free." This will be investigated in the British Pound case study.

Figure 16-3   Risk/Reward Profile: Long Calendar Spread

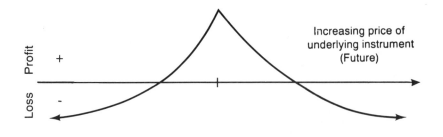

British Pound Case Study

The chart of the British Pound in Figure 16-4 shows a large Head & Shoulders Bottom. The long-term upside measuring objective on the December 1991 futures chart is 1.8100.

Figure 16-4   Large Head & Shoulders Bottom

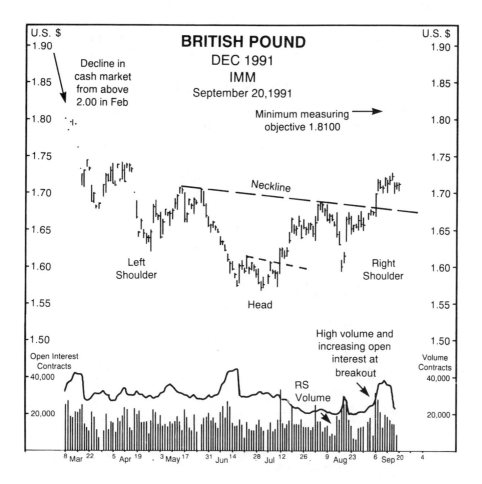

The most recent three weeks of price activity is enlarged in Figure 16-5. A look at the chart shows that a small H&S *Top* could form! A price rally on Monday, September 23, would fill a Pattern Gap at 1.7180 and possibly form a right shoulder. This is the very short-term technical expectation. If the high of the potential head at 1.7284 is not taken out, an H&S Top would be very possible, near term.

Can two Head & Shoulders formations—one bullish and one bearish—be active on a chart at the same time? Yes. The approximate downside measuring objective of the small topping pattern would bring quotes back to the price area of the neckline on the very large H&S Bottom. Thus, short term, a selloff is very possible before a resumption of the longer term uptrend.

An Elliott Wave count is found in Figure 16-6. It shows that five waves to the upside can be counted from the 1.5670 low on the December futures chart. A Wave 2 correction should be underway. Once finished, a 3 of ③ of III to the upside should occur. This count fits nicely with the classical bar charting outlook of short-term bearish and long-term bullish.

Figure 16-5   Possible Head & Shoulders Top

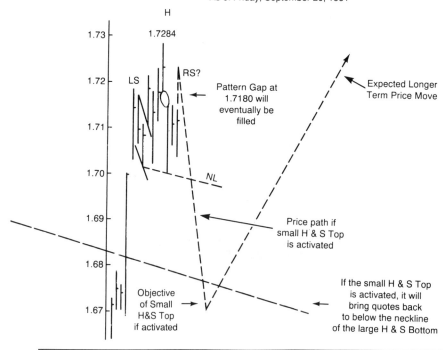

BRITISH POUND
DECEMBER 1991
IMM-DAILY CHART
As of Friday, September 20, 1991

Figure 16-6   Elliott Wave Count: Downward Correction Beginning

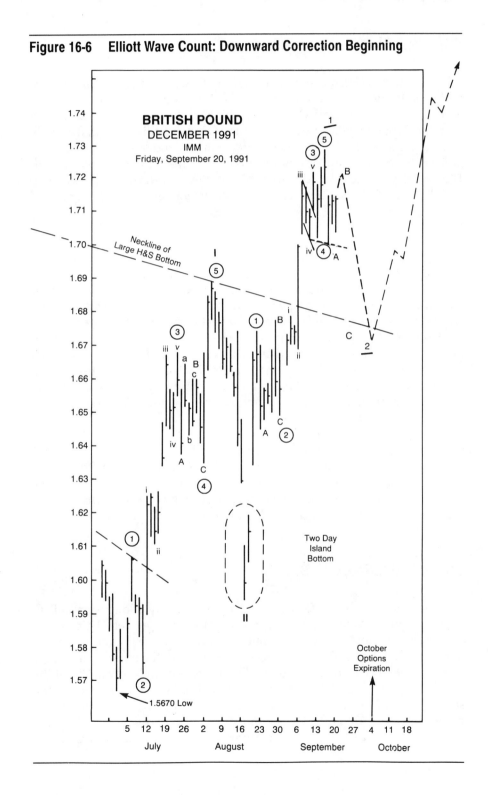

TRADING PLAN:

A long calendar spread using call options will be investigated. The October option series uses the December future as its underlying instrument. The options expire on Friday, October 4. This is only 11 calendar days from Monday, September 23. The at-the-money October British Pound (BP) calls will be the short leg of a contemplated long calendar spread. The more deferred December British Pound calls will be the long leg of the spread. This strategy would take advantage of expected near-term weakness in the British Pound followed by a resumption of the longer-term bull market.

Monday, September 23

A gap open to the upside at 1.7254 occurred on the December future on Monday. This can be seen in Figure 16-8, which contains price activity through the October options expiration. The gap (above Friday's high of 1.7140) was another Pattern Gap that should be filled. An aggressive trader, well aware of the unlimited risk, would investigate selling the at-the-money 1.7250 October calls. They were trading at 0.0146, normally referred to as 146 points. The minimum price fluctuation in British Pound futures and options on the IMM is 0.0002; each 2 points equals 12.50$US. If the British Pound then sold off in price—to fill the gap at Friday's high of 1.7140—a long 1.7250 call in the more distant December option series would allow the trader to leg into a long calendar spread.

In late trading on Monday, if quotes were trading above 1.7284, the gap would have to be reclassified as a Breakaway variety because quotes would have moved to new price highs, above 1.7284 (Figure 16-8). A Breakaway Gap is very dynamic and does not have to be filled. If a strong close above 1.7284 was probable, the bearish short-term strategy of writing the October calls must be abandoned. A small day trade loss would result.

DIAGONALIZING THE SPREAD

In determining a strategy for which call options to buy, a long-term bullish trader might consider purchasing an out-of-the-money call. This would diagonalize the spread. If the call option is purchased at a premium of equal to or less than the nearby at-the-money option sold, the trader would own a call for free. The British Pound would have to remain below 1.7250 at the October expiration in 11 calendar days. The entire 146-point premium of the short Oct 1.7250 call would have been used to purchase the out-of-the-money more deferred call. The December call option that was trading at a premium of less than 146 (the premium received from the short October) was the Dec 1.8000 call. It could have been purchased at 126 points going into the close of trading on September 23.

A major concern is whether the British Pound is likely to move up enough in price after the October call expires to make a long Dec 1.8000 call a good trade. The large Head & Shoulders Bottom is a very dynamic pattern that should meet its measuring objective of 1.8100. Since the spread is initially set up as a credit (146 - 126 = 20), if the October option does expire worthless, the overall spread would not be a loser no matter what the December future does.

The British Pound future did not move into new high price ground in trading on Monday, September 23. A diagonal calendar spread will be initiated on the close this trading session.

The spread being monitored in this case study will be short Oct 1.7250 calls versus long Dec 1.8000 calls. A typical brokerage house statement showing the option transaction and open trade status is shown in Table 16-1.

Table 16-1   Typical Brokerage Statement

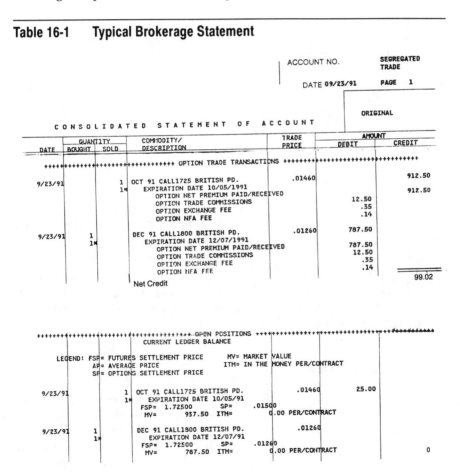

Options Derivatives

Table 16-2 lists the important derivatives for the Oct 1.7250 and the Dec 1.8000 British Pound call options.

Table 16-2   Options Derivatives—September 23, 1991

Dec British Pound Future = 1.7250

	Delta	Gamma	Theta	Vega	Implied Volatility
Oct 1.7250 call	.504	0.1	6.8	11.9	12.5
Dec 1.8000 call	.229	0.0	2.0	23.4	12.4

The theta of the nearby October option sold is 6.8. The theta of the December option bought is only 2.0. The October option will lose premium at greater than three times the rate of the December option. This is the good news; the potential bad news is that considerable risk exists in this position. The delta of the position is -.504 + .229 = -.275. This is clearly a bearish short-term position. The protection afforded by the long 1.8000 call will do little to offset the damage inflicted by the short 1.7250 call if the British Pound rallies.

Risk/Reward Analysis

Creating a risk/reward diagram involves an estimate of what the December option will be worth at the time of the October expiration. The estimated shape of the risk/reward diagram is seen in Figure 16-7.

Technical analysis will be very important in controlling the risk in this spread. A price increase above 1.7250 plus the 146 credit received from granting a call at that strike will begin to seriously damage the short-term bearish outlook. The maximum loss in this position is 730 points if a substantial price rally ensues.

Volatility Considerations

The vega (Table 16-2) of the long December option is larger than the vega of the October option sold. Thus, an increase in volatility should help the spread. The implied volatility in British Pound options has been relatively flat at 12.2 percent for the last four months. Thus, the current implied volatility of 12.4-12.5% cannot be stated as clearly too high or too low. More

**Figure 16-7   Estimated Shape of Risk/Reward Diagram
at Expiration of Nearby October Option**

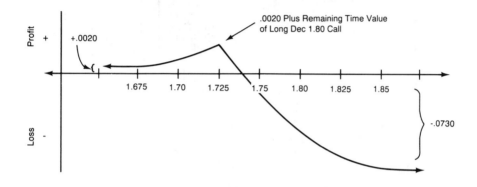

Diagonal Calendar Spread
Long 1 Dec 1.8000 BP Call at .0126
Short 1 Oct 1.7250 BP Call at .0146

important to this spread is the large negative delta (-.275). This means that directional considerations are more important than volatility considerations.

Tuesday, September 24

Volume and open interest statistics for Monday were available before trading began on the IMM Tuesday. Volume was low (10,814 contracts) and open interest declined 504 contracts. This confirmed the bearish nature of the price rally on Monday, September 23. The price activity in British Pound futures up to the October 4 options expiration can be seen in Figure 16-8.

The British Pound future opened exactly at Monday's low and moved lower in early U.S. dealing. Then a rally two hours into trading took quotes above Monday's high. The selloff in the U.S. Dollar in spot interbank dealing was attributed to the release of the U.S. Consumer Confidence Index showing a third straight monthly decline.

Technically, an Outside Range Day had formed. Although the H&S Top possibility was destroyed, this minor trend change indicator was another signal that the British Pound was trying to create a near-term price top on its chart. The staying power of the options spread allowed traders to with-

**Figure 16-8   Elliott Wave Revised Count
at Expiration of October Options**

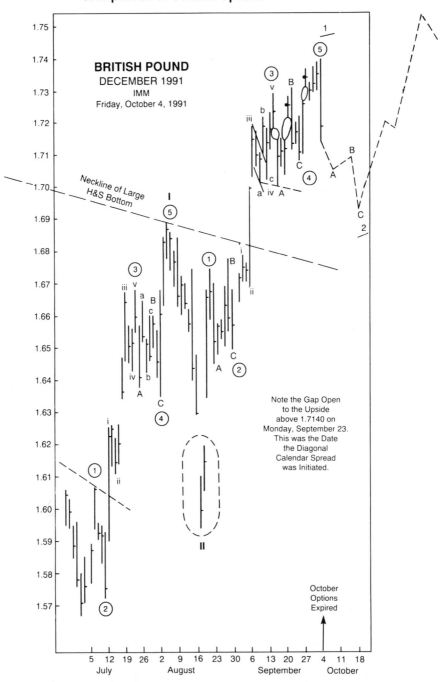

BRITISH POUND
DECEMBER 1991
IMM
Friday, October 4, 1991

Neckline of Large
H&S Bottom

Note the Gap Open
to the Upside
above 1.7140 on
Monday, September 23.
This was the Date
the Diagonal
Calendar Spread
was Initiated.

October
Options
Expired

stand the price rally. But the location of Tuesday's close would be important. A settlement above Monday's high of 1.7280 would make a short-term bearish view suspect.

News that the president of the U.N. Security Council had set a deadline for Iraq to release weapons inspectors who had been detained started a selloff in the IMM foreign exchange futures. The price down move in Sterling not only took out the day's low, but continued down to close the Pattern Gap at Friday's high of 1.7140. The weak close at 1.7132 created a Key Reversal Day. The technical expectation was that a lower low than the Key Reversal low of 1.7116 would be seen.

Monday, September 30

The Key Reversal high of Tuesday, September 24 did move the British Pound lower. But a gap open to the upside on Monday, September 30 put the British Pound near-term bearish options strategy in jeopardy once again. The opening price can be seen as the dot on the left side of the daily price bar in Figure 16-8. A price above 1.7396 at expiration would eliminate any profit potential from the short Oct 1.7250 call. The gap at Friday's high of 1.7268 must be classified as a Breakaway variety by virtue of the Monday 1.7338 close in new high price ground.

Volume will be the key as to the likelihood of a selloff to fill the gap at 1.7268. Volume greater than 19,000 contracts would be high, and the gap would not be expected to be filled; volume below 12,000 would be low, and an excellent possibility would exist that the British Pound would sell off the remainder of the week.

When released, total British Pound volume of only 10,281 contracts was very low. A selloff did occur on Tuesday to close the gap. Even lower volume occurred on Tuesday, Wednesday and Thursday. Together with the relatively flat open interest, a trader would (nervously) maintain the short October call leg. The highest the December British Pound traded was 1.7384 (intraday) on Thursday. The short Oct 1.7250 call position remained (though barely) in profit territory—and would, as long as the expiration price on Friday was below 1.7396.

Friday Expiration: October 4

The release of the U.S. unemployment figures on Friday morning was the fundamental report awaited by all financial instrument dealers. As often happens, at first look at the gross headline numbers, the markets reacted incorrectly. A brief surge took the December British Pound figure from its opening at 1.7344 to 1.7400. (See Figure 16-8). Upon deeper examination, a different fundamental conclusion surfaced. The rally proved to be a brief time/price relationship. The price highs were quickly rejected by the marketplace and quotes headed south.

The settlement price on the December future was 1.7186. The Oct 1.7250 calls expired worthless. The diagonal calendar spread trader was able to keep the entire 146-point credit from the October calls written. The Dec 1.8000 call settled at 88 points. This call could be held in anticipation of the large H&S Bottom pattern eventually working.

Another note of interest: The spot British Pound had a New York close on Friday, October 4, of 1.7350. Compared to the December future settlement price of 1.7186, this meant that the future (forward) was trading at a substantial discount to the spot. This basis relationship provided an added fillip to the now bullish stance of the holder of the long Dec 1.8000 calls.

OUTCOME OF LONG DECEMBER CALLS

Figure 16-9 shows what transpired after the October option series expired. It also contains a revised Elliott Wave count. The huge price rally that was forecasted from the large Head & Shoulders Bottom did indeed occur. The Dec 1.8000 call had an intrinsic value of 146 points based on the December British Pound futures close of 1.8146 on Friday, December 6, 1991.

SUMMARY

To summarize, the short nearby leg of a calendar spread did prove effective in capturing profit from a corrective price move. This was true even though the Elliott Wave count needed to be revised. The longer-term technical outlook, both from an Elliott Wave standpoint and classical bar charting, did allow the long deferred leg in the calendar spread to also contribute profit. This ideal situation is not easy to find, but this case study, as with all the others in this book, was not created after the fact!

Figure 16-9   Elliott Wave Count at Expiration of December Options

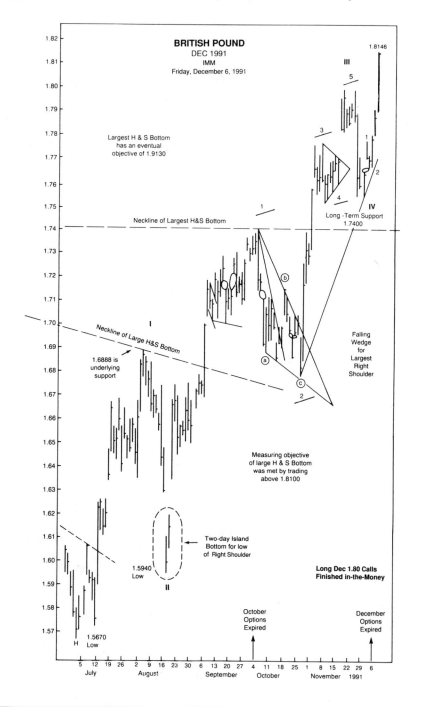

BRITISH POUND
DEC 1991
IMM
Friday, December 6, 1991

1.8146

III

5

3

1

2

IV

Long -Term Support
1.7400

Largest H & S Bottom
has an eventual
objective of 1.9130

4

1

Neckline of Largest H&S Bottom

b

Neckline of Large H&S Bottom

I

Falling
Wedge
for
Largest
Right
Shoulder

1.6888 is
underlying
support

a

c

2

Measuring objective
of large H & S Bottom
was met by trading
above 1.8100

Two-day Island
Bottom for low
of Right Shoulder

Long Dec 1.80 Calls
Finished in-the-Money

1.5940
Low

II

October
Options
Expired

December
Options
Expired

1.5670
Low

H

5 12 19 26 2 9 16 23 30 6 13 20 27 4 11 18 25 1 8 15 22 29 6
July   August   September   October   November   1991

CHAPTER 17

VOLATILITY CHARTS

The same human emotions that produce classic price patterns on a chart create changes in implied volatility. There is no reason why technical analysis should not be applied to implied volatility charts. The implied volatility charts in this chapter are mini-case studies. They are included as food for technical thought.

The implied volatility charts of gold futures options in Figure 17-1 illustrate a typical phenomenon. This chart shows the difference between tops and bottoms on implied volatility charts of markets that the public likes to trade from the long side. The emotion that creates an increase in volatility premiums often creates spiked tops. Both the put and call charts in Figure 17-1 exhibit traditional Head & Shoulders Top configurations. This is not unusual.

But lows on physical market (gold, grains, livestock) implied volatility charts tend to be long and drawn out. This is akin to the Rounding Bottom formation in classical bar charting. Markets do have personalities, and these traits quite often extend into implied volatility considerations.

The plot of U.S. Treasury bond futures implied volatility in Figure 17-2 is included to illustrate an actual situation. A Chicago Board of Trade member was asked in February what he was doing in the T-bond market. His answer: I'm buying volatility. Asked why, his response was: Because it's low. Queried again as to his view of the market in March, he answered: I bought volatility because I thought it was low . . . and it moved lower. The moral is how do you know when to buy volatility? It looked low for two months!

Figure 17-2 does show that eventually T-bond implied volatility did move substantially higher. But waiting for the Rounding Bottom to end was agonizing. As usual, timing is critical to an options trader.

Figure 17-1 (A)   Implied Volatility Chart
August 1987 Comex Gold Futures Options

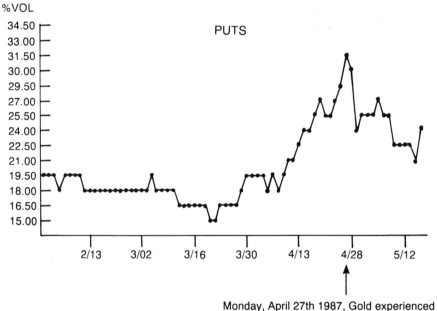

Monday, April 27th 1987, Gold experienced
a wild trading day. The range was 45$/ oz.
This formed a huge Outside Range Week!

Figure 17-1 (B)   Implied Volatility Chart
August 1987 Comex Gold Futures Options

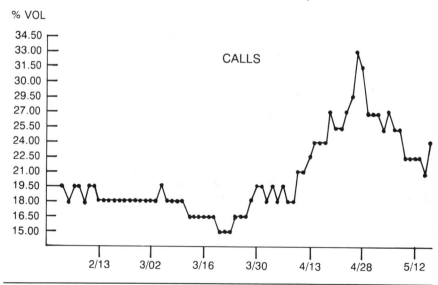

**Figure 17-2   Implied Volatility Charts
September 1987 T-Bond Futures Options**

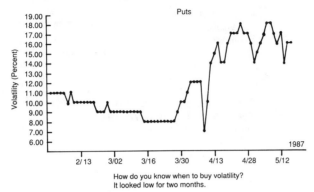

How do you know when to buy volatility?
It looked low for two months.

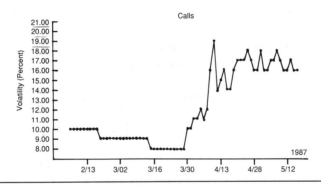

OEX IMPLIED VOLATILITY

The emphasis in this book has centered on options on futures. What about implied volatility charts of the popular S&P 100 (OEX) Index options traded on the Chicago Board Options Exchange? Figure 17-3(A) is an attempt by a crude dot matrix printer to plot both call and put implied volatilities on a single chart. A's are used for puts and B's for calls. If the call and put volatility readings are so close together that the printer cannot physically print both an A and B, an asterisk is posted.

The first reaction when looking at Figure 17-3(A) is that the individual implied volatility plots must be much different. Indeed, when separating the two charts in Figure 17-3(B), the shapes are quite different. Implied volatility in the OEX call options began increasing at an earlier date than the puts. This reflected a bullish bias on the part of the speculative public.

An important historical note must be added to Figure 17-3. This was the period early in 1987, prior to the crash in October of that year. Since then, equity market implied volatility characteristics have often reflected fear

**Figure 17-3(A)   Implied Volatility Chart (Both Puts & Calls)
June 1987 S&P100 Index Options**

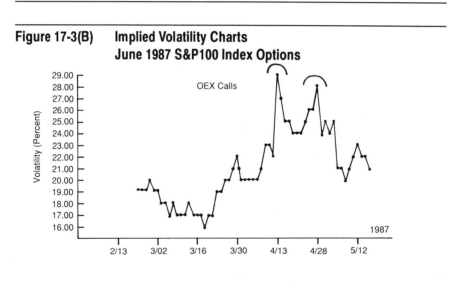

**Figure 17-3(B)   Implied Volatility Charts
June 1987 S&P100 Index Options**

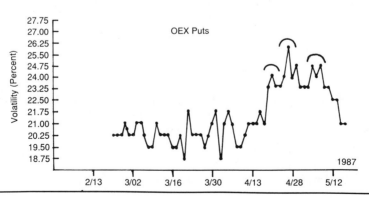

rather than greed. Put implied volatility escalates when equity prices hit an air pocket. The perception is that price protection against another crash is necessary. This pumps up the implied volatility of put options.

Figure 17-3(B) continues to illustrate the tendency of spike tops. The call chart has a Double Top and the put chart traced out a Head & Shoulders Top.

SOYBEAN IMPLIED VOLATILITY

When implied volatility soars as in the case of soybean options (Figure 17-4), a bull market price blowoff is probably in progress. A technically oriented trader would be watching for any minor signs of a top on the price chart. These would include any of the four minor trend change indicators: Key Reversal, Outside Range Day, Inside Range Day or Mid-Range Close posting. The aggressive options strategy is to write calls.

A straight volatility trader may want to write delta-neutral straddles and try to keep the position delta neutral. But technical analysis of the price chart

**Figure 17-4   Implied Volatility Chart (Both Puts & Calls)
                 November 1987 Soybean Futures Options**

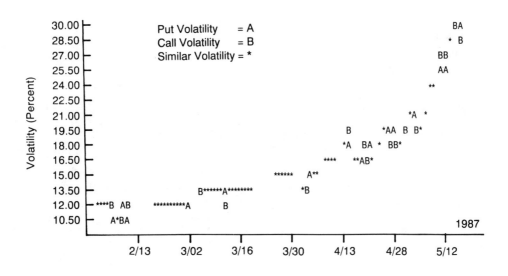

will allow an aggressive trader to position himself with respect to implied volatility *and* price considerations.

U.S. INTEREST RATE VOLATILITIES

The remaining figures in this chapter contain volatility charts that encompass the extreme agitation seen in many markets during the time of the October 1987 world equity market crash. Figures 17-5 through 17-7 illustrate the flight to quality into both short-term time deposits and long-term fixed instruments. Historical and implied volatility soared.

**Figure 17-5   Implied Volatility Chart (Both Puts & Calls)
June 1987 IMM Eurodollar Futures Options**

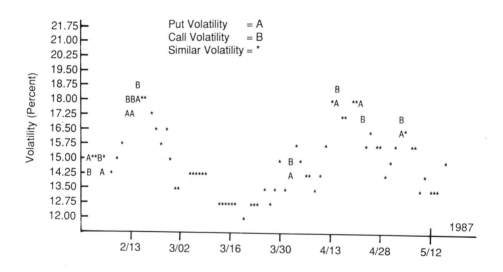

Question: What is your definition of "High" and "Low" implied volatility?

Figure 17-6   Volatility Charts: IMM Eurodollar Futures Options

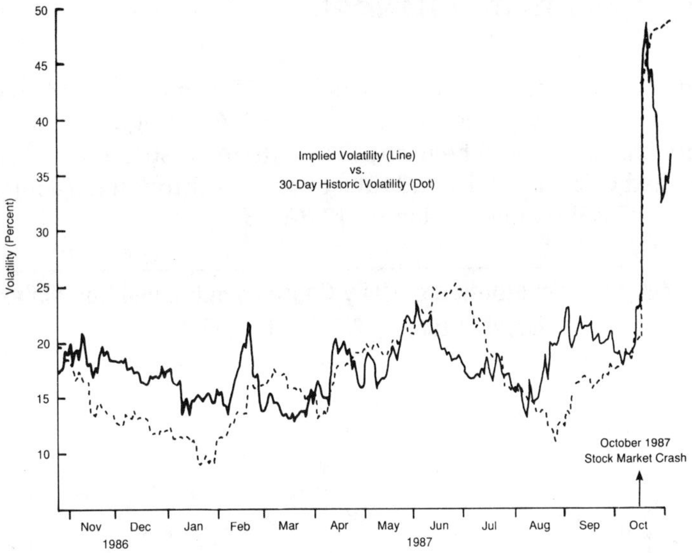

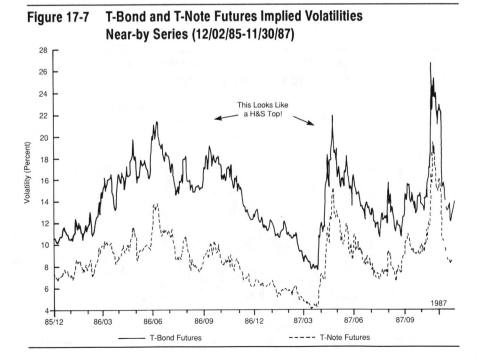

Compare your answer to the question posed in Figure 17-5 to Figure 17-6 showing what happened to implied volatility during the flight to quality following the world equity market collapse later in 1987.

**Figure 17-7   T-Bond and T-Note Futures Implied Volatilities
Near-by Series (12/02/85-11/30/87)**

DISTRIBUTION OF PRICE AND IMPLIED VOLATILITY CHANGES

Of particular interest to any options trader is: How much is implied volatility likely to change from one day to the next? A histogram showing daily volatility changes would be useful. The extreme distribution in both price and implied volatility in T-bond futures options through the equity market crash of 1987 is illustrated in Figure 17-8A&B.

Figure 17-8 (A)   **Distribution of Daily Changes in Implied Volatilities T-Bond Futures (12/02/85-11/30/87)**

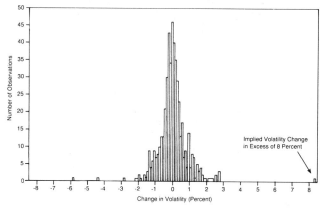

Figure 17-8 (B)   **Distribution of Daily Changes in Near-by Futures Price T-Bond Futures (12/02/85-11/30/87)**

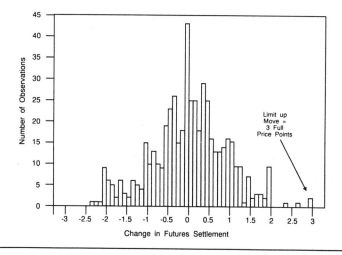

RELATED MARKETS?

The astronomic surge (and fall) in the S&P 500 futures options volatility is shown in Figure 17-9. To show that the world is emotionally connected (especially on the same trading floor), Figure 17-10 is included. Approximately 75 feet away from the S&P 500 pit on the floor of the Chicago Mercantile Exchange is the live cattle pit. The carnage in the S&Ps during the October '87 debacle was also reflected in an unwillingness to write live cattle options. Implied volatility soared and collapsed!

Figure 17-9   S&P 500 Volatilities (11/86 - 10/87)

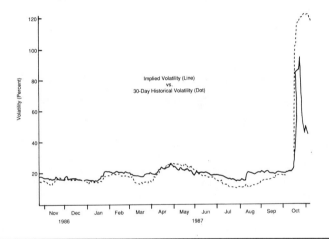

Figure 17-10   Live Cattle Volatilities (11/86 - 10/87)

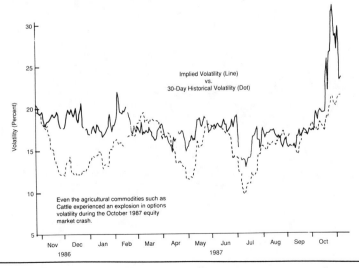

CHAPTER 18

PUTTING IT ALL TOGETHER

A technical trader must always be ready to react and readjust a trading strategy based upon subsequent price activity. The cocoa case study in this chapter is a flow of technical analysis and options strategies over time.

A technician is often on the sidelines waiting for something classic to appear on a chart. Discipline dictates that the correct trade is no trade. This was the initial condition of the cocoa market in mid-1990.

September and December '90 Cocoa Case Study

The technical condition of the September 1990 cocoa chart in Figure 18-1 can be summarized as follows:

1. Classic underlying support at the mid-April high of 1395 has been violated.

2. Three reversals of the minor price trend are in place.

3. Reversal point 2 at the 1252 price low in early May is a benchmark low. It does not represent classic underlying support. But a price bounce from this level on declining volume would be bearish; an excellent potential for the development of a Head & Shoulders Top would exist.

4. Current volume parameters are:

   - 12,000+ = high

   - 8,000– = low

Figure 18-1   Watch for Additional Technical Development

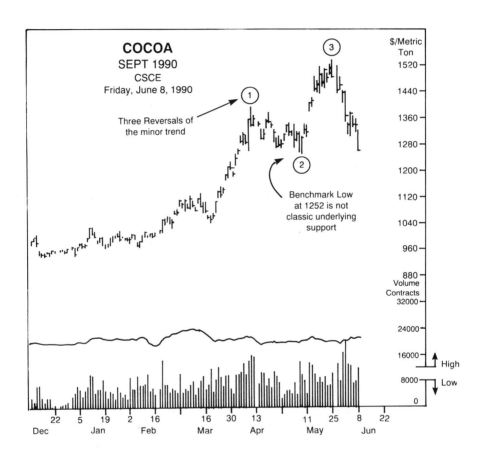

Given

1. Size of cocoa futures contract = 10 metric tons.

2. Minimum price fluctuation = 1$/metric ton = 10$US per contract.

3. September 1990 cocoa settlement price = 1265.

4. Options prices for the close June 8 were:

```
COCOA (CSCE) 10 metric tons; $ per ton
Strike      Calls—Settle          Puts—Settle
Price    Sep-c Dec-c   Mr-c   Sep-p Dec-p  Mar-p
1100      179   219    ....    14    32     34
1200      110   150    157     38    67     52
1300       56   110    128     91   115    123
1400       33    67     80    163   172    175
1500       16    45     50    251   258    245
1600       10    32     40    345   345    ....
Est. vol. 2,225; Thur vol. 688 calls; 332 puts
Open interest Thur; 15,276 calls; 18,433 puts
```

Trading Plan

None immediately. A technician would be monitoring the cocoa chart for any low volume price rally emanating from the area of the 1252 low.

Five Weeks Later: July 13, 1990

Figure 18-2 shows that a price rally did occur in the September cocoa futures. The current technical overview is:

Figure 18-2   A Price Rally Ensued

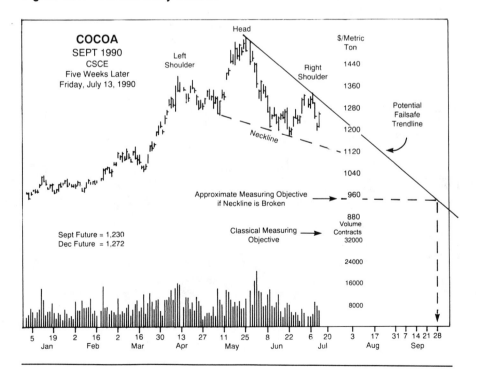

1. The price rally in late June/early July was on declining volume. This is ideal for a right shoulder in a possible Head & Shoulders Top.

2. The highest volume in the last three weeks occurred on a price down day; this is bearish.

3. Open interest in cocoa futures is remaining relatively flat. This means that "fuel" to sustain a price move is not leaving the market. It is a favorable technical situation for a sustainable price move.

4. A Head & Shoulders Top would be activated on the September cocoa chart if a close is registered below the neckline. Application of the traditional height measuring objective would forecast a move down to approximately 930. But an H&S Top cannot be expected to retrace more than the price move that preceded it. Thus, the minimum downside target would be the 940 level.

5. If the potential H&S Top is activated and the fail-safe trendline is not violated, the downside measuring objective would be reached no later than September 26. This dictates the option expiration to use: the December 1990 series with an expiration date of November 2 would be appropriate.

6. September cocoa settled at 1230; December cocoa settled at 1272.

Figure 18-3   Initiate a Vertical Bear Put Spread

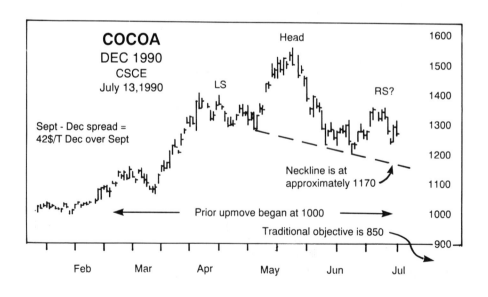

DECEMBER COCOA

The December 1990 cocoa chart (Figure 18-3) looks similar. Cocoa is in a normal carrying charge environment with the December contract trading 42$/T over the September. The approximate location of the neckline on the December chart is 1170. The downside target would be 1000 (retracing the prior upmove) and 850 as determined by application of the standard H&S Top measuring objective.

Options prices for Friday, July 13, 1990 were:

COCOA (CSCE) 10 metric tons; $ per ton

Strike	Calls—Settle			Puts—Settle		
Price	Sep-c	Dec-c	Mr-c	Sep-p	Dec-p	Mar-p
1000	232	280	....	1	8	21
1100	131	197	239	7	25	37
1200	48	130	172	21	58	70
1300	13	78	113	86	115	111
1400	3	49	80	173	161	155
1500	1	28	55	271	256	225

Est. vol. 1,482; Thur vol. 477 calls; 508 puts
Open interest Thur; 17,753 calls; 17,915 puts

Figure 18-4   Risk/Reward Diagram: Vertical Bear Put Spread
Long one Dec 1100 put
Short one Dec 1000 put

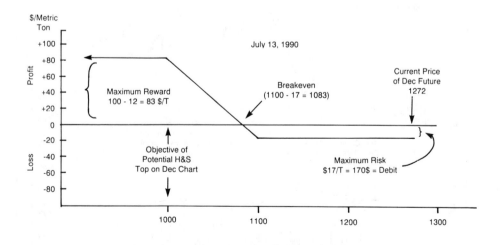

Trading Plan

A straightforward approach to trading the potential Head & Shoulders Top is a vertical bear put spread. Using options strikes on either side of the 1170 neckline on the December chart creates the following spread:

	Delta	Implied Volatility
Long Dec 1100 put at 25	−.181	32.8
Short Dec 1000 put at 8	+.075	32.2

This is a debit spread of 17$/T per one-lot spread. Two or more contracts must be used to allow for follow-up flexibility.

Delta Analysis

$$-.181 + .075 = -.106 \text{ (per one-lot spread)}$$

The risk/reward diagram of this strategy is shown in Figure 18-4.

Figure 18-5   Potential Symmetrical Triangle

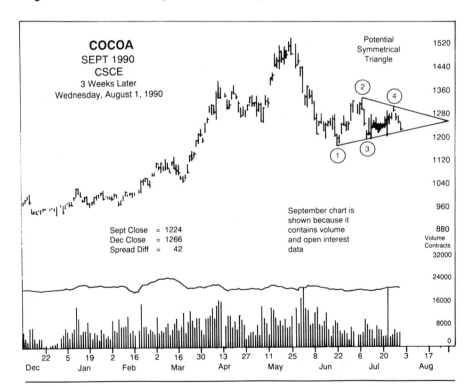

Follow-Up

August 1, 1990

Figure 18-5 shows that the potential right shoulder of the Head & Shoulders Top has evolved into a Symmetrical Triangle price pattern on the September chart. This is the most liquid contract month and the only chart on which most mechanically reproduced chart services plot volume and open interest. The December chart contains the same price pattern. The formation of a Triangle does not necessarily change the bearish outlook. Specifically:

1. The high probability direction for the Triangle breakout (75 percent) is to the downside.

2. The two breakout levels from the Triangle on the September chart are 1300 and 1220.

3. The height of the Triangle as measured at reversal point 2 is 140$/T.

4. If the breakout occurs to the downside, application of the height measuring objective would project to a target of approximately 1080 on the September chart and 1140 on the December chart.

5. Options prices for August 1, 1990 were:

COCOA (CSCE) 10 metric tons; $ per ton

Strike	Calls–Settle			Puts–Settle		
Price	Sep-c	Dec-c	Mr-c	Sep-p	Dec-p	Mar-p
1000	231	270	....	1	4	20
1100	119	184	....	1	18	28
1200	38	115	160	12	44	56
1300	2	65	95	72	96	91
1400	1	37	65	171	154	161
1500	1	20	55	271	254	251

Est. vol. 823; Tues vol. 390 calls; 89 puts
Open interest Tues; 18,661 calls; 17,697 puts

Trading Plan

1. Vertical bear put spreads can be held. The current status of the original spread (per one-lot) is:

			Delta
Long one Dec 1100 put	=	18	−.147
Short one Dec 1000 put	=	4	+.045
Value of Spread	=	14	

The spread was originally placed at a debit of 17$/T, so the open trade loss is 3$/T per one lot spread. Implied volatility fell to 28.9 percent (expected in a Triangle).

2. For traders not already positioned, two additional strategies can be considered:

   • at-the-money, relatively delta-neutral long straddle

   • put ratio backspread to place positions with a directional bias to a downside breakout

3. Traders must examine an implied volatility chart and determine if premiums appear to be low or high with respect to implied volatility. The current reading of implied volatility below 30 percent is not high. The cocoa volatility chart in Figure 18-6 shows that implied volatility increased into the high 30s in September.

4. The closest to a delta-neutral 1:1 long straddle is:

		Delta	Implied Volatility
Long one Dec 1300 call	at 65	+.448	29.2
Long one Dec 1300 put	at 96	−.533	28.6

This is a debit spread of 161$/T per one lot spread. As usual, two or more contracts are required for follow-up flexibility.

Delta Analysis

$$+.448 + -.533 = -.085 \text{ (per one-lot spread)}$$

The risk/reward diagram of the long straddle is found in Figure 18-7.

Figure 18-6   Cocoa Options Implied Volatility

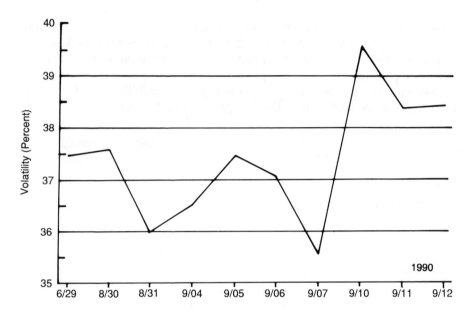

Figure 18-7   Risk/Reward Diagram of Long Dec 1300 Straddle
at Expiration

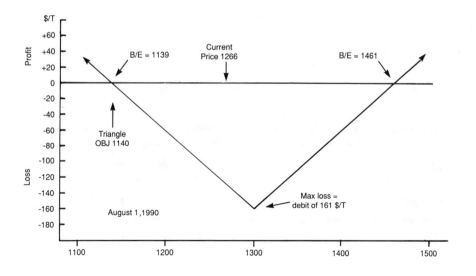

ANOTHER TRADING PLAN

An aggressive technical trader would want to design an option strategy with a greater negative delta. This would bias the trade in favor of the Triangle formation most often (75 percent) being a continuation pattern rather than a reversal pattern.

Skewing the strategy in favor of the higher probability of a downside price breakout results in the following put ratio backspread:

			Delta	Implied Volatility
Short one Dec 1400 put at 154	=	154 credit	+.718	26.5
Long two Dec 1300 puts at 96 x2	=	192 debit	−.533	31.1
		38$/T debit		

Delta Analysis

$$+.718 + (-.533 \times 2) = -.348$$

A tabular risk/reward matrix of the put ratio backspread is seen in Table 18-1. The graphic risk/reward profile is seen in Figure 18-8.

Table 18-1   Risk/Reward of Put Ratio Backspread at Expiration

Price at Expiration	1000	1100	1200	1250	1300	1350	1400	1450
Value of short 1 1400 put	−400	−300	−200	−150	−100	−50	0	0
Value of long 2 1300 puts	+600	+400	+200	+100	0	0	0	0
Spread result	+200	+100	0	−50	−100	−50	0	0
Initial debit	−38	−38	−38	−38	−38	−38	−38	−38
Net result	+162	+62	−38	−88	−138	−88	−38	−38

Figure 18-8   Graphic Risk/Reward Profile of Put Ratio Backspread at Expiration

Short one Dec 1400 Put

Long two Dec 1300 Puts

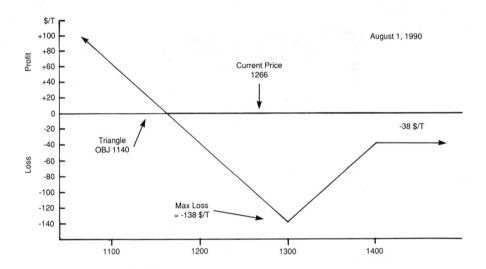

TRIANGLE BREAKOUT

1. On Thursday, August 2, 1990, both September (Figure 18-9) and December cocoa just barely closed out the downside of their respective Triangles. Volume was lackluster (4,912) and open interest (-81 contracts) showed long liquidation.

2. More decisive (bearish) readings were seen on the continuation of the price down move on Friday, August 3. Volume swelled to 10,355 and open interest expanded (+36 contracts). This data has not yet been posted on the chart in Figure 18-9.

3. Triangle objectives:

   • September cocoa = 1080

   • December cocoa = 1145

4. Symmetry for a Head & Shoulders Top is quickly disappearing with the extended amount of price congestion and time spent on the possible right shoulder. But the Triangle breakout is bearish.

5. September cocoa settled at 1176; December cocoa settled at 222.

6. Options prices for August 3, 1990 were:

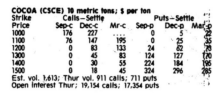

COCOA (CSCE) 10 metric tons; $ per ton						
Strike	Calls—Settle			Puts—Settle		
Price	Sep-c	Dec-c	Mr-c	Sep-p	Dec-p	Mar-p
1000	176	227	....	0	5	22
1100	76	147	195	0	25	35
1200	0	83	133	24	62	78
1300	0	45	83	124	127	170
1400	0	30	55	224	184	195
1500	0	18	45	324	296	285

Est. vol. 1,613; Thur vol. 911 calls; 711 puts
Open interest Thur; 19,154 calls; 17,354 puts

Figure 18-9   Triangle Breakout

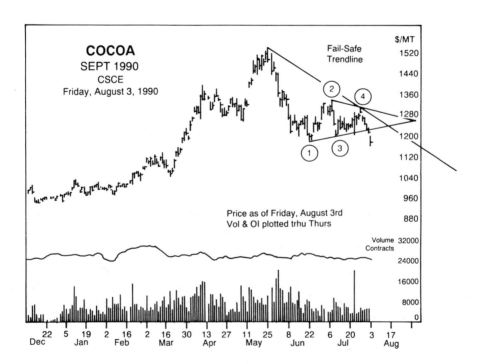

Trading Plan

1. Remove one-half of losing leg on all positions.

2. Wait for pullback to overhead resistance (reversal point 1 in the Triangle) to exit from remaining one-half of the losing leg.

3. Construct a down-sloping fail-safe trendline as seen in Figure 18-9.

Three positions have been posed in this case study: the original vertical bear put spread, a long straddle, and a put ratio backspread. One-half of the losing leg in each of these positions will be removed.

1. Original vertical bear put spread:

Buy one Dec 1000 put at 5
(for a "loss" of 8 - 5 = +3$/T)
Note that the 1000 put declined in value over time
although price declined from 1271 to 1222.

Present Position

Long two Dec 1100 puts (at 25 vs 25 now)
Short 1 Dec 1000 put (at 8 versus 5 now)
Open trade profit = 0 X 2 + +3 = + 3
Overall situation* = +3 + +3 = +6

2. Original long straddle:

Sell one Dec 1300 call at 45
(for a loss of 45 - 65 = -20$/T)

Present Position

Long two Dec 1300 puts (at 96 versus 127 now)
Long one Dec 1300 call (at 65 versus 45 now)
Open trade profit = +31 X 2 + -20 = +42
Overall situation* = +42 + -20 = +22

3. Original put ratio backspread:

Buy one Dec 1400 put at 184
(for a loss of 154 - 184 = -30)

Present Position

Long two Dec 1300 puts (at 96 versus 127 now)
Open trade profit = +31 X 2 = +62
Overall situation* = +62 + -30 = +32

* Overall situation = Current open trade profit or loss + profit or loss just realized because one-half of the losing leg was removed at the Triangle breakout.

By Friday, August 10, one week after the Triangle breakout, the strategy remained unchanged. No pullback to the Triangle took place nor had the Triangle objective been reached.

TRIANGLE OBJECTIVE MET

Friday, August 17, 1990

Figures 18-10 and 18-11 show that the Symmetrical Triangle measuring objectives were achieved on both the September and December cocoa charts. A very severely down-sloping neckline of an H&S Top was penetrated on the September cocoa chart but not on the December chart. The trading strategy is to take partial profits (because the Triangle objective was met) and lower the stop-loss point to above the price high on August 10. The options prices for August 17 and details of the three positions are:

COCOA (CSCE) 10 metric tons; $ per ton

Strike	Calls—Settle			Puts—Settle		
Price	Dec-c	Mar-c	Ma-c	Dec-p	Mar-p	May-p
900	244	....	....	4	20	....
1000	154	213	....	14	26	32
1100	90	142	172	44	55	55
1200	40	88	113	105	100	96
1300	21	54	67	193	167	150
1400	11	38	50	271	....	233

Est. vol. 307; Thur vol. 542 calls; 221 puts
Open interest Thur; 10,399 calls; 12,506 puts

1. **Original vertical bear put spread:**

   Sell one Dec 1100 put at 44
   (for a profit of 44 - 25 = +19$/T)

   Present Position

   Long one Dec 1100 put (at 25 vs 44 now)
   Short one Dec 1000 put (at 8 vs 14 now)
   Open trade profit = +19 + -6 = +13
   Overall situation* = +13 + +3 + +19 = +35

2. **Original long straddle:**

   Sell one Dec 1300 put at 193
   (for a profit of 193 - 96) = +97)

Present Position

Long one Dec 1300 put (at 96 vs 193 now)
Long one Dec 1300 call (at 65 vs 21 now)
Open trade profit = +97 + -44 = +53
Overall situation* = +53 + -20 + 97 = +130

3. **Original put ratio backspread:**

Sell one Dec 1300 put at 193
(for a profit of 193 - 96 = +97)

Present Position

Long one Dec 1300 put (at 96 vs 193 now)
Open trade profit = +97
Overall situation* = +97 + -30 + +97 = +164

* Overall situation = Current open trade profit or loss + profit or loss of removing one-half of losing leg at the Triangle breakout + profit just realized because the Triangle objective was met.

Figure 18-10   Triangle Objective Met

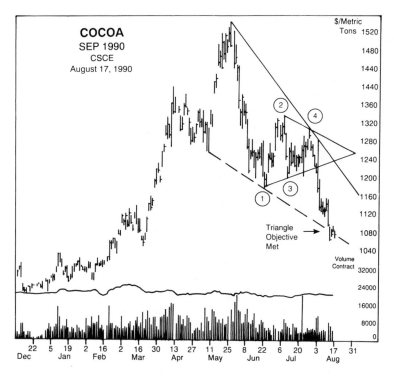

Figure 18-11   Triangle Objective Met

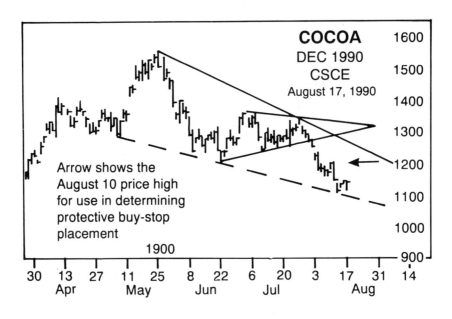

Arrow shows the
August 10 price high
for use in determining
protective buy-stop
placement

COCOA
DEC 1990
CSCE
August 17, 1990

1900

Outcome

Figure 18-12 shows that the fail-safe trendline was violated with a vengeance. In fact, an apparent upside breakout from a bullish Falling Wedge occurred. All remaining positions would be liquidated. The options prices for Friday, August 24, were:

COCOA (CSCE) 10 metric tons; $ per ton

Strike	Calls—Settle			Puts—Settle		
Price	Dec-c	Mar-c	Ma-c	Dec-p	Mar-p	May-p
1000	384	370	408	3	14	22
1100	287	273	315	6	17	29
1200	193	238	228	18	33	42
1300	125	175	170	48	61	84
1400	70	125	123	88	100	137
1500	43	86	84	162	230	198

Est. vol. 2,864; Thur vol. 118 calls; 51 puts
Open interest Thur; 10,941 calls; 12,583 puts

Figure 18-12 Fail-Safe Trendline Violated

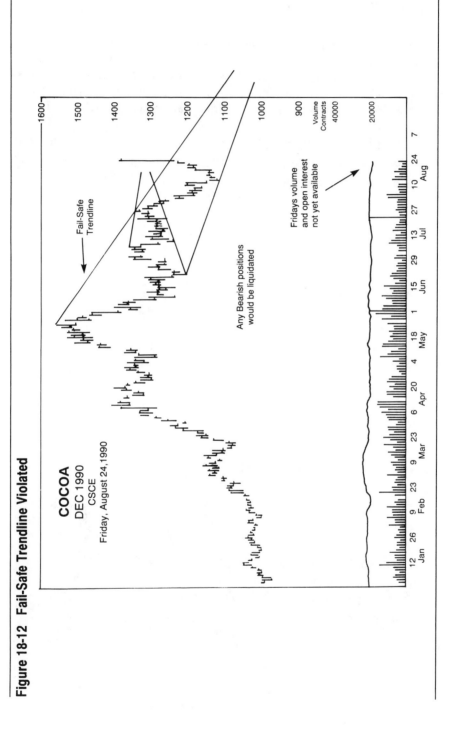

SUMMARY

Two accounting methods are available to summarize the outcome of the cocoa options campaign. The debits and credits at each decision node can be summed or the net profit or loss (P/L) of each transaction can be accumulated. First, all remaining options are liquidated (stopped out) as of the close Friday, August 24. Both accounting approaches are detailed.

1. **Original vertical bear put spread:**

    Sell one Dec 1100 put at 6 (6 - 25 = -19)
    Buy one Dec 1000 put at 3 (8 - 3 = +5)
    Result = -14 (receive a credit of 3)

Recap

	Debit/Credit		P/L
1. Original debit –17 x 2 =	–34	(July 13)	—
2. Triangle breakout	– 5	(August 3)	+ 3
3. Triangle objective	+44	(August 17)	+19
4. Stopped out	+ 3	(August 24)	–14
	+ 8$T		+ 8$T

2. **Original long straddle:**

    Sell one Dec 1300 put at 48 (48 - 96 = -48)
    Sell one Dec 1300 call at 125 (125 - 65 = +60)
    Result = +12 (receive credit of 173)

Recap

	Debit/Credit		P/L
1. Original debit –161 x 2 =	–322	(August 1)	—
2. Triangle breakout	+ 45		–20
3. Triangle objective	+193		+97
4. Stopped out	+173		+12
	+ 89$T		+89$T

3. **Original put ratio backspread:**

    Sell one Dec 1300 put at 48 (48 - 96 = -48)
    Result = loss of 48 - 96 = -48 (receive credit of 48)

Recap

	Debit/Credit		P/L
1. Original debit	− 38	(August 1)	-—
2. Triangle breakout	−184		−30
3. Triangle objective	+193		+97
4. Stopped out	+ 48		−48
	+ 19$T		+19$T

The word "campaign" is appropriate to describe this cocoa case study. The chart was first examined on June 8 and deemed to be worth monitoring in case a Head & Shoulders Top was developing. When this seemed highly likely, five weeks later, vertical bear put spreads were initiated on July 13.

The possible right shoulder then evolved into a Symmetrical Triangle. This dictated the addition of either long straddles or more directional put ratio backspreads on August 1. The breakout of the Triangle in the expected direction on August 3 prompted removal of one-half of the losing leg.

When the Triangle objective was met, partial profits were taken August 17 on the various options strategies. Mental stop-loss orders were then placed on the cocoa chart. When these protective stops would have been activated, all remaining options were liquidated on August 24.

This book has attempted to offer insights into the interaction of technical analysis and options strategies in actual market situations. Technical analysis is an art, not a science. And the particular options strategies suggested in each case study were not necessarily optimal. The hope is that this book has created a greater insight into the combination of these two powerful diciplines.

APPENDIX A

GLOSSARY

A-T-M. At-the-money. The option strike which is closest to the current settlement price of the underlying instrument.

Backspread. An options position where more options have been purchased than sold.

Benchmark Low. A recent low price posting on a chart. A benchmark low is *not* considered underlying support to a classical bar chartist.

Benchmark High. A recent high price posting on a chart. A benchmark high is *not* considered overhead resistance to a classical bar chartist.

Blowoff volume. Extraordinarily high volume. This is a warning signal that the price trend is in the process of exhausting itself, at least temporarily. Prices often move violently in the opposite direction after blowoff volume.

Butterfly Spread. The sale (purchase) of two options and the purchase (sale) of one option of the same type and expiration at a higher strike and the purchase (sale) of one option of the same type and expiration at a lower strike.

Cabinet. A trade between two parties, each of whom is liquidating an existing options position. The price of a cabinet quote is usually less than one regular option tick.

Calendar Spread. An options spread in which the short term option is sold and the longer term option is purchased. Both options are of the same type and exercise price. A calendar spread is a specific form of a time spread.

CBOE. Chicago Board Options Exchange. The first exchange to trade options on exchange listed U.S. equities. The CBOE was created by the

Chicago Board of Trade; its first trading floor was the old members' cafeteria in 1972!

CBOT. Chicago Board of Trade. All U.S. domestic futures exchanges were allowed to trade options on futures in October 1982.

CME. Chicago Mercantile Exchange.

Cluster of Closes. Three or more relatively unchanged closes in a volatile instrument. A significant price move would be expected soon.

Comex. Commodity Exchange Incorporated.

Credit Spread. Option spread which brings funds into an account. The net sale proceeds are greater than the net purchase cost.

Debit Spread. Option spread which requires funds to be paid out from an account. The net purchase cost is greater than the proceeds received from the net sale.

Delta. Change in the theoretical price of an option given a one-point change in the price of the underlying instrument. Mathematically, delta is the first derivative of a theoretical option pricing model with respect to price.

Fail-Safe Trendline. Trendline constructed tangent to the price extremes at the head and right shoulder of a Head & Shoulders reversal formation. The fail-safe trendline is used for placement of protective stop-loss orders.

First Delivery Day. First day on which delivery can occur. On the CBOT physical contracts, this is the first business day of the expiration month.

GLOBEX. Global Exchange. The electronic trading exchange developed by the Chicago Mercantile Exchange. Dealing on GLOBEX commenced the evening of Thursday, June 25, 1992 in the U.S. This officially began the trading "day" of Friday, June 26.

Gamma. Change in the delta of an option given a one-point change in the price of the underlying instrument. Mathematically, gamma is the second derivative of an options pricing model with respect to price.

Gap. No overlap in price on a chart from one trading session to the next. Gaps occur most frequently on a chart encompassing one time zone only. A gap would only be found on a 24-hour spot foreign exchange chart over a weekend or major worldwide holiday.

Pattern Gap. Occurs within a congestion area or trading range; quickly closed.

Last Traverse Pattern Gap. Occurs on the "last traverse" across a congestion area prior to a breakout; does not have to be filled.

Breakaway Gap. Occurs at the beginning of a new price move; associated with the penetration of a trendline; does not have to be closed. The higher the volume on the trading session that created the gap, the less likely the gap will be closed.

Measuring Gap. Found during a rapid, straight-line price move; represents the mid-point of a dynamic price trend.

Exhaustion Gap. Occurs at the end of a price move; quickly filled. Exhaustion Gaps tend to be "wide" gaps and generate blowoff volume.

Suspension Gap. Created when no overlap in price occurs between the evening CBOT T-bond session when trading is suspended and the resumption of trade the following morning. A Suspension Gap is also possible between the electronic trading hours on GLOBEX and the resumption of trading during regular open-outcry trading hours. Suspension Gaps must be classified as one of the four main types of gaps.

Horizontal Spread. Spread consisting of options with the same strike but different expiration dates.

Head & Shoulders (H&S). A five-point reversal formation that may be found at either a top or bottom. The H& S formation is considered the most classic of all bar charting price patterns.

IMM. International Monetary Market. The division of the Chicago Mercantile Exchange that trades currency and interest rate futures.

Inside Range Day. Lower high and higher low than the previous trading session. This price posting should act as a minor trend change indicator. After a price up move, it forecasts a lower daily low the next trading session. After a price down move, it forecasts a higher daily high the next trading session.

Intrinsic Value. The value of an option if expiration were to occur immediately.

IOM. Index and Options Market. The division of the Chicago Mercantile Exchange that trades stock index futures and options on the CME products.

ITM. In-the-money. A call option with a strike price below the current price of the underlying instrument. A put option with a strike price above the current price of the underlying instrument. These options have intrinsic value equal to the amount they are in-the-money.

Key Reversal Day. A new contract high (or low) with a close below (or above) the previous close on a bar chart. It forecasts a lower low (or higher high) than the Key Reversal Day's posting. A Key Reversal posting on a chart is only a minor trend change indicator.

MMI. Major Market Index. An index of 20 high quality "blue chip" U.S. equities. This index is highly correlated with the Dow Jones Industrial Average. The American Stock Exchange trades options on the MMI. The CBOT trades an MMI future and futures options.

Mid-Range Close. A price posting for a close on a bar chart that is equidistant between the high and low for that bar. The direction of the price trend coming into the Mid-Range Close has been neutralized. Quotes are expected to reverse direction, at least temporarily.

Minor Trend Change Indicator. Either a Key Reversal, Inside or Outside Range Day, or Mid-Range Close price posting on a chart.

Open Interest. For futures or options, open interest is the summation of all unclosed purchases or sales at the end of a trading session. Long Open Interest = Short Open Interest = Total Open Interest.

OEX. Ticker symbol for the popular S&P100 stock index option traded on the Chicago Board Options Exchange.

O-T-M. Out-of-the-money. A call option with a strike price above the current price of the underlying instrument. A put option with a strike price lower than the current price of the underlying instrument. Neither option has any intrinsic value.

Outside Range Day. Higher high and lower low than the previous trading session. This price posting should act as a minor trend change indicator. After a price up move, it forecasts a lower daily low the next trading session. After a price down move, it forecasts a higher daily high the next trading session.

Put-Call Ratio. Number of puts traded for every 100 calls. This ratio is sometimes used in a contrary sense. If a high level of puts are being traded, for example 77 puts to every 100 calls, a bullish outlook results.

Ratio Spread. An options position where the number of longs is unequal to the number of shorts.

Resistance. A former price low on a chart; resistance is always overhead on a chart.

Resumption. Quotes *resume* trading after a trading halt. This occurs in a market that has a split trading session designed to cover a 24-hour "day". A resumption of trade can also occur after a temporary limit price move expires.

Rho. The derivative of an options pricing model that measures the sensitivity of an option's theoretical value to a change in interest rates.

Serial Expiration. Options that expire in the months in between the quarterly expiration series. Serial expiration options are exercisable into the next futures contract.

Short-Dated Options. Options that will exercise into the next futures contract. For example, June, July and August short-dated D-Mark options on the IMM exercise into the September futures contract.

Straddle. Options position of long (short) a call and long (short) a put with both options having the same underlying instrument, expiration date, and exercise price.

Strangle. Options positions of long (short) a call and long (short) a put with different exercise prices (typically out-of-the-money) and the same underlying instrument and expiration date.

Support. A former price high on a chart; support is always underlying on a chart.

Suspension. Trading is *suspended* when a break in a split trading session occurs. A suspension of trade also takes place when a limit price move on a futures contract occurs.

Synthetic. The combination of long or short positions in the underlying instrument and long or short positions in an option to create an instrument with similar risk/reward characteristics to the actual instrument. For example, a position of long the underlying instrument plus a long put is a synthetic long call.

Theta. Time decay; the change in the theoretical price of an option as time passes. Theta is not a linear function and can only be used over a short time period, i.e., a few days.

Time Spread. Options spread consisting of two options of the same type and expiration price, but different expiration months. A calendar spread is a type of time spread in which the short term option is sold and the longer term option is purchased.

Vega (Also known as Zeta, Lambda or Kappa). Change in the theoretical price an option given a one percent change in implied volatility. Mathematically, Vega is the first derivative of an options pricing model with respect to volatility.

Vertical Spread. Spread consisting of options with the same underlying instrument, type and expiration date, but different strikes.

Vertical Bear Spread. Long an option with a higher strike and short an option with a lower strike of the same type and expiration.

Vertical Bull Spread. Long an option with a lower strike and short an option with a higher strike of the same type and expiration date.

Volatility. One standard deviation of daily price change in one year; expressed as a percent.

    Historical - Measures the actual past variability of any price series. It can be computed over any number of trading days (e.g. 20, 30, 60, 120, 250, etc.)

    Implied - Measures the price variability that the market place is imputing into the underlying instrument. Implied volatility is "back calculated" using an options pricing model.

Volume. For futures and options, the number of contracts traded each trading session. The published volume figure represents one side of the trade only. Buy Volume = Sell Volume = Total Volume.

XMI. Ticker symbol for the popular Major Market Index option traded on the American Stock Exchange. An option on the CBOT MMI future was launched on the CBOT in October 1991.

Wedge. A classic bar chart continuation pattern consisting of two converging trendlines which both slope either up or down.

Rising Wedge -   A bearish price pattern in which both converging boundary lines slope up. When activated by a close below the lower boundary line, a new price low is forecasted.

Falling Wedge - A bullish price pattern in which both converging boundary lines slope down. When activated by a close above the upper boundary line, a new price high is forecasted.

APPENDIX B

THEORETICAL OPTIONS PRICING MODEL

Five input variables are typically used to calculate a theoretical fair value price for a futures option. Dividend payments are an additional variable if the underlying instrument is an equity. A modification of the Fisher Black and Myron Scholes model (1973) referred to as the Black Model (1976) will be used to calculate theoretical option values and the various mathematical derivatives in this book. This is the formula used by the Chicago Mercantile Exchange in its Options & Alternatives software. The formula for a futures call option premium (C) is:

Table B-1

$$C = e^{-rt}[FN(d_1) - SN(d_2)]$$

where:

$$d_1 = [Ln\,(F/S) - (V^2t)/2]/(V\sqrt{t})$$
$$d_2 = [Ln\,(F/S) - (V^2t)/2]/(V\sqrt{t})$$

r	=	Risk-free interest rate (i.e., T-bill rate)
t	=	Time to expiration (in fractions of a year; i.e., 90 days = t = 90/365 ≅ .25)
F	=	Price of underlying futures contract
S	=	Strike price of option contract
Ln	=	Natural logarithm
e	=	Base of the natural logarithm
V	=	Annualized estimated volatility of the underlying futures prices
$N(\,)$	=	Area under the curve of a normal distribution to the left of (d_1) or (d_2) respectively

The five inputs to the model are:

1. price of the underlying instrument
2. strike price
3. time to expiration
4. interest rate
5. volatility

The outputs from the model are:

1. theoretical fair value of the call
2. derivatives such as delta, gamma, theta, vega, rho.

In order to engage in any "what if" analysis, the options trader must have access to software/hardware to run a theoretical options pricing model.

An options pricing model is also used to determine the implied volatility in an option. The five inputs now include the existing price instead of a volatility figure. The output is the implied volatility that the marketplace is inputting into that option.

The implied volatility derived from "working the model backwards" is for a single option only. Implied volatilities can be calculated for both puts and calls of different strikes and expiration dates. The trader must always be aware of with which implied volatility figures he is working.

APPENDIX C

OPTIONS PRICING DIAGRAMS

Figure C-1   Plot of Intrinsic Value of a 100 Strike Call at Expiration

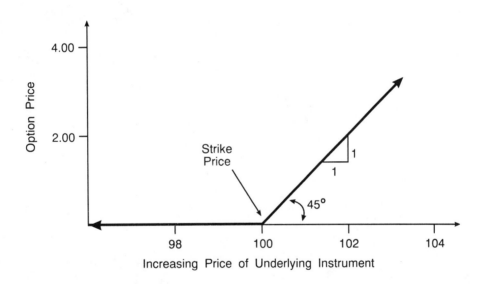

**Figure C-2   Plot of Theoretical Value of a 100 Strike Call
with Time Remaining until Expiration**

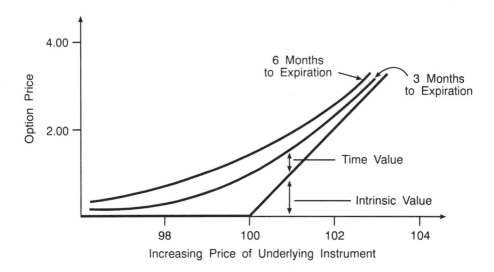

Note that the maximum time value occurs when an option is at-the-money.
Implied volatility changes will affect this option to the greatest extent. This
can be measured using the options derivative vega.

Figure C-3   **Option Deltas**

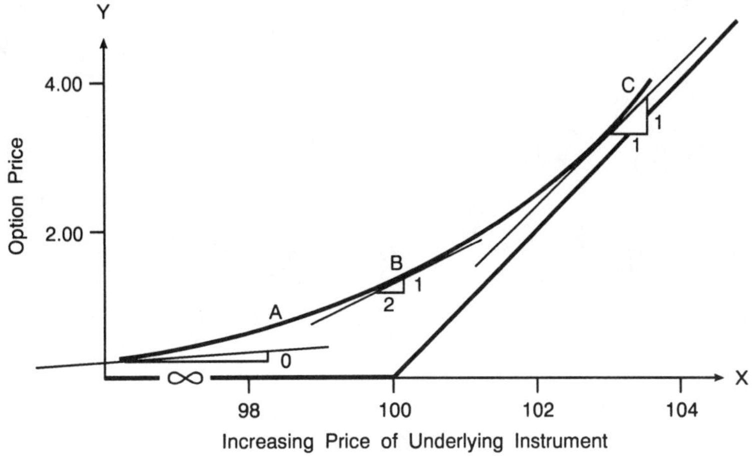

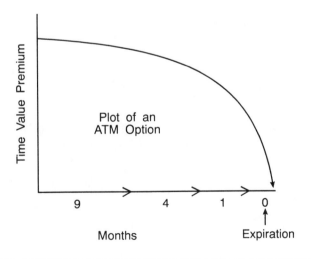

	Delta	=	Slope	=	Change in Y/Change in X at point:
A.	Delta	=	0/∞	=	0.0
B.	Delta	=	1/2	=	0.5
C.	Delta	=	1/1	=	1.0

Figure C-4   **Plot of Theoretical Time Decay Curve**
                        of an at-the-Money Option

Theta   =   Slope of the decay curve

APPENDIX D

WHERE TO OBTAIN THE DATA

CHICAGO EXCHANGES
Chicago Mercantile Exchange
"MercLine" 312-930-8282

Available by 4:00 AM Chicago Time
(and often earlier)

Selected Financial Instrument Contracts:

	Price Codes*			Vol & OI Codes*		
	Futures	Calls	Puts	Futures	Calls	Puts
Eurodollars	321	463	465	320	464	466
S&Ps	127	459	461	126	460	462
D-Mark	345	359	361	346	360	362
Swiss Franc	349	363	365	350	364	366
Japanese Yen	347	367	369	348	368	370
British Pound	341	371	373	342	372	374

* Codes are for regular trading hours

Electronic Trading Hours (GLOBEX)

	Price	Vol & OI
D-Mark	719	718
Swiss Franc	919	918
Japanese Yen	819	818
British Pound	801	800

Chicago Board of Trade
and MidAmerica Commodity Exchange
"Midis-Touch" 900-990-2268 ($0.65/minute)

T-Bond Information

14#	=	5:00 PM cleared volume
2200#	=	Preliminary volume and open interest (available 8:30 AM Chicago time)
2600#	=	Actual volume and open interest (available noon Chicago time)
2700#	=	Evening price range
12#	=	Resumption range

Technicians not able to access a U.S. 900 number can call the CBOT to adquire
a personal identification number to use in obtaining the statistics.

Chicago Board Options Exchange
1-800-OPTIONS

NEW YORK EXCHANGES
Coffee, Sugar and Cocoa Exchange
212-938-2847

Commodity Exchange
212-938-9020 Info Line (volume 9:00 AM; open interest 11:00 AM CST)

212-432-2821 Cotton and Orange Juice (10:00 AM CST)
212-432-7274 Options
212-839-9038 FINEX

New York Futures Exchange
212-938-4946 (not recorded)

New York Mercantile Exchange
212-938-0064 Fastfacts
212-656-8423 volume and open interest

OTHER EXCHANGES
Kansas City Board of Trade
816-753-1101

Minneapolis Grain Exchange
612-338-6212 (not recorded)
612-340-9438 (prices only)

INDEX

Kenneth H. Shaleen is President of CHARTWATCH, an international research firm to the futures industry, and CHARTWATCH CAPITAL MANAGEMENT, a managed global technical trading corporation. Among the many services offered by CHARTWATCH and CHARTWATCH CAPITAL MANAGEMENT are:

- A weekly technical research report *CHARTWATCH*
- Daily telephone market updates covering financial instrument futures
- Technical analysis videotapes
- Technical analysis course presentations
- Managed trading accounts

Please direct all inquires concerning any of these services to:

CHARTWATCH
Fulton House 1700
345 North Canal Street
Chicago, IL 60606 USA
Telephone: 312-454-1130
Fax: 312-454-1134

About the Publisher

PROBUS PUBLISHING COMPANY

Probus Publishing Company fills the informational needs of today's business professional by publishing authoritative, quality books on timely and relevant topics, including:

- Investing
- Futures/Options Trading
- Banking
- Finance
- Marketing and Sales
- Manufacturing and Project Management
- Personal Finance, Real Estate, Insurance and Estate Planning
- Entrepreneurship
- Management

Probus books are available at quantity discounts when purchased for business, educational or sales promotional use. For more information, please call the Director, Corporate/Institutional Sales at 1-800-PROBUS-1, or write:

Director, Corporate/Institutional Sales
Probus Publishing Company
1925 N. Clybourn Avenue
Chicago, Illinois 60614
FAX (312) 868-6250